A PRACTICAL AND SPIRITUAL GUIDE

Careering

Old Definition: Single company, until age 65 and retirement
New Definition: Multiple jobs, companies and industries;
entirely new occupations throughout life

HOW TO FIND AND MAINTAIN MEANINGFUL WORK IN TODAY'S ECONOMY

✝✝✝

DANA WALLACE GOWER   VENARD PAUL DEAN

 DG Publishing
Copyright © 2015 by Dana Gower and Paul Dean
www.careeringbook.com
https://www.facebook.com/careeringbook

First Edition
ISBN: 978-0-9905494-0-6

The Career Network Ministry
Professional Development, Mentoring and Networking

 ### St. Andrew the Apostle Roman Catholic Church, Apex, NC

 ### Catholic Charities of the Diocese of Raleigh, NC

 ### Knights of Columbus, Council 6650, Cary, NC

Special thanks to the above organizations for their help and inspiration in producing this book.

It is our sincere hope that people of all faiths, even those who do not associate with any faith or religion, benefit from our efforts.

All net proceeds from this book, and from book-related fundraising activities, go to charitable purposes including job initiatives for the unemployed and under-employed.

ACKNOWLEDGEMENTS

Many wonderful people contributed to this work. We cannot say enough good things about them. Thank You!

Ideas, Content Contributors and Editors

Martin Brossman Success Coach/Speaker/Trainer/Author & Social Media Expert

John McKenna Principal Owner at Apex Business Success

John M. O'Connor President, CareerPro, Inc.

Sandra Bueno Personal Performance Coach and Founder MPowered 4Life Academy

Sterling Fulton Life Strategist, Founder of Your Space to Thrive & Author of the Brain Trust Planner

Graham Crispin CEO, XelAqua, Inc.

Deb Oronzio Career Coach/Trainer, Self–Empower Coaching

Christy Rain, JD Administrator/Freelance Writer

Sheyenne Kreamer CEO, Triangle Solutions Alliance, Inc.

Bob Stapleton Executive Coach/Human Resource Consulting and Vice President, Dorcas Ministries

Donna Flick Financial and Non–Profit Professional

Bill Spreitzer Senior Partner/Performance Coach –Excellerate Solutions

Eric Hamo Financial Services Professional

Richard Jordan Senior Human Resources/Talent Management Executive, Founder & Owner, Strengthening Talent

Anthony V. Edwards Senior Software Architect Professional

Bladimir Flores Business Development Mgr., Loan Consultant ATP Investments

Nadine Fulton Retired public school educator, Teacher of the Year at two schools, in South Carolina (1989) and in Ohio (1999)

Alisha Ramsey TV Host, Video Producer, Storyteller & Flea Market Junkie

Graphics/Formatting

Elena Skrinak Owner, Creative Director, SkrinakCreative

Magdalena Adic Graphic Artist, mag.ing.tech.lign

TABLE OF CONTENTS

Catholic Charities
OF THE DIOCESE OF RALEIGH *Providing Help. Creating Hope.*

Dear Brothers and Sisters in Christ,

In a country with so much wealth, so many thriving businesses, and such leadership in the area of technological advances, it is unfortunate that there is so much economic disparity and such widespread "disengagement" within the workforce. Despite the economic recovery, unemployment and especially under-employment remain higher than we should accept.

In his address to the people gathered in St. Peter's Square in May 2013, our most Holy Father Pope Francis stated "Work is fundamental to the dignity of a person. Work, to use a metaphor, 'anoints' us with dignity, fills us with dignity, makes us similar to God, who has worked and still works, who always acts (cf. Jn 5:17); it gives one the ability to maintain oneself, one's family, and to contribute to the growth of one's own nation."

Additionally, it is unacceptable that many Americans are not fully satisfied with their employment or career situation. Our faith teaches us that in addition to work providing dignity, work is intended to be fulfilling for the worker.

We are fortunate that two parishioners of the Diocese of Raleigh, who are also members of the Knights of Columbus, Mr. Dana Gower and Mr. Paul Dean, from St. Andrew the Apostle Parish in Apex, have brought to publication this practical guide to networking and career advancement. In this volume, they capture the major issues and strategies for effective personal 'career management'. They challenge workers to be better workers and employers to be better employers through relationship building, life-long learning, and faith. This is an outline for dignified, rewarding work across all segments of our society. I am especially grateful for the spiritual reflections and real-world examples contained in this book, so that those striving to improve their work lives can have the grounding, in concrete terms, of faith and hope as they move forward to find a fulfilling path for their careers.

It would be well for us to embrace the principles in this book and to employ them for ourselves. In doing so, we can eliminate the structural causes of unemployment/under-employment and help people find more meaning in their work. Our Catholic teaching calls us to fulfillment in our work lives, and this can be accomplished with initiatives, such as those contained in this book.

Sincerely In Christ,

Gary S. Skinner
Executive Director
Catholic Charities of the Diocese of Raleigh

Saint Joseph – the Worker;
persistent,
devoted to family,
loving and kind,
obedient to God,
head of the Holy Family, and
a compassionate and caring man.

PREFACE - PAUL'S STORY

LAYOFFS! WHY IS THIS HAPPENING TO ME AND MY FAMILY, AGAIN?

It was May 2, 2001, and I had just been informed that my job was eliminated. This was my third and final layoff episode from Nortel Networks. I called my wife, Barbara, gave her the news and went home. Barbara picked up the kids from school and told them on the way home that Daddy lost his job today, so he is going to be sad when you see him. Our 7 year-old daughter Andrea, replied, "When I get home, I'll help him find it". Barbara explained what a job was and what it meant to lose a job. Andrea said she understood that, and also what her daddy needed to do in order to get a new job.

When they drove up the driveway, I was in the yard looking at trees and flowers, pondering things. Andrea jumped out of the car and said, "Daddy, don't come in the house yet… I've got something to do!" I usually receive a hug when she comes home, but this time she was on a mission. She darted into the house. Barbara gave me a longer-than-usual hug, and I asked her … "What's up with Andrea?" She said she was not really sure… but that she explained to her about my job loss and that I would be sad. About 10 minutes later, Andrea opened her bedroom window and yelled, "Ok, Daddy, you can come in now. But, Mommy, you can't come in, this is just for Daddy."

"Applekation"

I went upstairs and Andrea's bedroom door was closed. There was a freshly torn piece of notebook paper taped to the door. In crayon, she had written the words "Knock Before You Enter." I knocked and heard Andrea say, "Come in." She was sitting at her small table and then stood up and said, "Hello, Mr. Dean, please have a seat." She pointed to a small chair, and I crouched down and sat down with her on the other side. She handed me a piece of paper, on which, written with a crayon in her best first grade spelling, was the word "Applekation." I soon figured it to be "Application", and I played along by writing down my name and address. She acted so professional. She sat with her hands folded and waited. I handed it to her and she said, "Thank You! Now I have three questions you need to answer for this job." She had taken time to write the following three questions on a piece of paper:

1. *Do you want to love me and be taking care of me?*
2. *Do you want to be my daddy, and we will always be together, even in heaven?*
3. *Do you want to do all the fun things we like to do together?*

As I read these questions, I had one of those wonderful emotional moments. I felt good all over. Words really couldn't describe it. Losing my job totally left my mind—I just felt great! I wrote "Yes" next to each question in the space provided and handed it back to her. She read each response and put a check mark next to each one of my answers. She then stood up and said, "Congratulations, Daddy! You have a new job!" I gave her a big hug and said, "Thank You, Dear!" I will take that moment with me until the day I depart this life.

Course Correction

When one door closes, another one opens. Going through the hallway between can be filled with feelings of loss, confusion, fear and frustration. Paul's story about being laid-off and his young daughter's keen insights provided him with purpose, clarity and direction. Jobs change. Paul awakened to the awareness that nothing else mattered more than the love and care of his family and faith. But how do you care and provide for family while being fulfilled with meaningful and purposeful work?

Sometimes, career transition provides you with an enormous opportunity to pursue and do work that is significant, fulfilling, and rewarding through passion and purpose. Be strong, courageous, and resolute.

"Your Career Is Our Cause"

May God bless you and your loved ones

DANA AND PAUL

Careering

**How to Find and Maintain Meaningful Work
In Today's Economy**

Dear Lord,

I ask for Your wisdom regarding my future, knowing that
You give to everyone liberally and without reproach.

I ask in faith, without doubting, expecting You to give me
direction in every area of my life, especially in helping me
to understand my divine purpose.

Help me to be passionate and of good courage
as you lead me in the way I should go.

Father, give me the strength to follow the pathway of faith - not
the path of fear - and one of power, love and a sound mind.
Amen

WHY YOU SHOULD READ THIS BOOK

In the Spirit of Love and Embracing Change
Dana and Paul, October 2015

The days of working for a single employer for an entire lifetime are gone. Things have changed dramatically—especially within corporate America. As members of the Baby Boomer generation, we have witnessed these changes from the beginning.

Similar to our parents before us, we went into the workplace thinking we would stay with one employer for our entire career. We've had to transform ourselves—the hard way—into a new way of thinking about employment. During his twelve years of corporate work, Paul experienced three layoffs in four years, each time showing loyalty by faithfully returning— only to be laid off again. Apart from feeling scared, he was also worried about his family's livelihood. Dana, after providing seventeen years of loyal and productive service, was dropped one day, without explanation.

This book will give you confidence, inspiration and insights into how you and your loved ones can navigate the New World of Work. Professionals of all ages will benefit from reading it. This is not your typical career, self-help or motivational book. The rich content will guide you in cultivating and maintaining professional relationships, help you identify your natural talents, including key weaknesses to improve upon and provide you with career branding tools, all under a faith-based belief system to ensure your success. Each chapter includes an Introduction, Quotation, Reflection, Prayer, and Activities Worksheet. This book contains stories of real people and includes many of our own life's lessons. Having worked for large corporations before transitioning to self-employment, we understand the nature of corporate jobs. We also know the trials and tribulations of owning our own businesses. We've been hired, fired and re-hired, promoted, transferred, rewarded,

> ## Ca•reer•ology
> *Your perspective on a situation is crucial to your success. Be sure to make good things happen from 'bad' situations.*

reprimanded, congratulated, even insulted and humiliated. We have felt emotions you may have experienced—frustration, happiness, sadness, anger, elation, and depression. Moreover, as directors of the Career Network Ministry at St. Andrews the Apostle Catholic Church in Apex, North Carolina, we've worked with many others who have been in the same situation. We know about the emotional and financial stresses on you and your family, especially during job transition.

For many of us change is tough. Additionally, the speed of change in business and organizations in today's New World of Work makes it challenging to know which direction will be appropriate for you in the years ahead. This book shows you how to take ownership of your career—and succeed—regardless of your circumstances. After all, we know first–hand it's not what happens to you, but oftentimes what you make of it that determines your direction and your success.

With all that we've seen and experienced, we want to help you to be better prepared than we were. Managing your career in the New World of Work is a test of endurance... accept it and take advantage of every opportunity.

The following chart shows how the work environment, mindset and transitory nature of employment, or 'The New World of Work', has evolved, requiring a lifetime lifecycle career management, free agent approach.

Lifetime Lifecycle Career Management	
Old Employee Model	**New Free Agent Model**
1. One Company, One Career 2+ Jobs, 1 Company and Career Until Ages 60 to 65.	**1. Portfolio Careers** 10+ Jobs, 5+ Companies and 2+ Careers Throughout Your Life.
2. Single Environment Permanent, Full-Time Employment with Benefits, Education and Training at One Firm.	**2. Variable Environments** Multiple Companies, Industries, Optional Career Paths and Diverse Work Arrangements. Limited Benefits from Companies.
3. Narrow Loyalties Employee and Company Very Loyal to Each Other.	**3. Broad Loyalties** Employee/Consultant's Loyalties Heavily Tied to Profession(s) and Network Contacts. Must Have 'Plan B' Jobs and Occupations as Backups.
4. Limited Commitment Choice to Be Fully Engaged with Company or Not.	**4. Full Commitment** Must Act Professionally and Demonstrate Competence in the Business, Technology and Human Dynamics at All Times.
5. Low Security Livelihood Determined Primarily by Boss and The Economy.	**5. More Security** Livelihood Determined Mostly by Achievements, Network and Successful Self-Marketing.
6. Robot Mindset Fit into Company's Mold – Don't Take Risks and Don't Stand Out.	**6. Creative Mindset** Innovations Important – Take Calculated Risks. Build a Strong Identity and Reputation, i.e. Personal Brand.
7. External Self–Worth Personal Identity Tied to Employer – Who You Worked for Was Very Important.	**7. Internal Self-Worth** Personal Identity Tied to Your Life and Career Purpose.

OUR RANT ABOUT THE 'NEW ECONOMY'

We have hope and offer help for a brighter future for our families and neighbors - especially children and grandchildren.

As Baby Boomers living in a country desperately trying to bring prosperity back en masse following the Great Recession that began in 2008, we offer only faith-based optimism with regard to the economic future of the United States. For much of America, a lack of financial security has significantly contributed to many of our problems, including higher rates of crime, domestic violence, excessive anxiety, illness, divorce, and even suicide.[1] We look forward to the day when our country regains its solid economic foundation, when anyone who is willing and/or able to work can find rewarding opportunities, and when we can all feel a sense of pride over the results.

Based on economic history, we should have seen a more robust rebound from the difficult times we've lived through since 2008. Given the structural changes of our economy and political climate, and despite improved economic headlines, it's hard to imagine any widespread, substantive progress without a new approach. The experience of most people remains relatively unchanged.

Consider some key social and economic indicators and characteristics that plague our country:

- Dependency/poverty levels are still extraordinarily high. According to the U.S. Census, 14.9%, or almost 50 million Americans were living below the poverty line in 2014.[2]
- Official unemployment rates are improved, but are distorted and still excessive—especially among younger people and older long-term unemployed adults. As of June 2014, the known number of unemployed workers not included in official statistics was 3.1 million.
- Under-employment is substantial, including fewer people working in well-paying middle-class jobs. Lower wage industries accounted for just 22% of jobs lost during the Great

Recession; however, lower wage industries represented a startling 44% of job growth over the past several years.[3] Forty percent (40%) of Americans with college degrees were not working in jobs requiring a degree, as of 2013.[4]

- A significant unknown is what impact will be seen on jobs, companies, and the economy from:
  o Millennials entering the workforce (those born from the early 1980's to early 2000's).
  o Immigration policies, and
  o Baby Boomers retiring (approximately 4 million are turning age 65 each year).[5]
- Dissatisfaction amongst many people with their jobs or workplaces is extraordinarily high. According to Gallup, 70% of American workers are not reaching their full potential.[6]
- Lack of patriotism, basic concern, and moral authority among numerous top organizational leaders is prevalent.[7] For example: Volkswagen, Enron, and Bernard L. Madoff Securities.
- Fear leading to constant battling between various political factions is stifling progress. Per Time/Business & Money, Washington dysfunction cost at least 2 million jobs in the U.S.[8]

A wide-spread lack of quality leadership among many businesses and governmental bodies for several decades seems to have taken its toll on our country.

"We believe that each and every one of us should take a servant–leader, spirit–filled approach to fix many problems in our country."
DANA AND PAUL

What do we mean by a servant-leader style, bottom-up, spirit-filled approach? We must take ownership of our individual circumstances, demand greater leadership, and work on better and broader relationship building. This can begin with truly knowing, loving and helping our neighbor as ourselves, i.e. more Americans doing more effective good deeds that provide conduits for service and contribution. These are basic tenets of the Catholic Church and core values fostered by the Founding Fathers of the United States. Despite the value that the Internet provides, people have become more disconnected than since modern communications emerged. This has led to distancing—emotionally and otherwise—both at home and in the workplace. Only when people are truly connected at a root, or foundational level, can community, commerce, and economics flourish.

✟✟✟

"Far and away the best prize that life has to offer is the chance to work hard at work worth doing."

THEODORE ROOSEVELT, JR. – 26TH PRESIDENT OF THE UNITED STATES

✟✟✟

We refer to St. Joseph throughout this book because of his obedience and persistence. He serves as a beacon for hope and guidance in the working world. Pope Francis has this to say about St. Joseph: "We celebrate the feast of St. Joseph the Worker. Joseph, the carpenter of Nazareth, reminds us of the dignity and importance of labor. This is where work is part of God's plan for the world; by responsibly cultivating the goods of creation, we grow in God's image. For this reason, the problem of unemployment urgently demands greater social solidarity and wise and just policies."[9]

> ## Ca•reer•ology
> *St. Joseph, the great protector of Jesus and Mary, is considered the Patron Saint of Workers and a role model for career and family success.*

We believe Pope Francis' message provides us with several incentives. First, we need to encourage all top leaders to become more proactive and concerned about the financial, physical, and emotional well-being of workers—a type of humanistic capitalism, if you will. Second, we need to work together to improve ourselves. This requires us to broaden and sharpen our skills, improve our physical/emotional conditioning, take charge of our career journey, and learn how to bring and maintain more passion into our work. Finally, we believe government leaders must ensure our policies support a strong, sustainable economy, along with rational and simplified regulations that uphold, defend and facilitate the just needs of businesses and workers alike.

The Pope is not alone in his plea. The Knights of Columbus, a Catholic fraternal service organization with over 1.8 million members[10], also has historic interests in helping workers and their families. Father Michael McGivney, founder of the Knights in Connecticut in 1882, acknowledged unemployment and lack of financial security as serious problems of the times. We see these issues, along with under-employment, as equally concerning today.

✝✝✝

"If we ever forget that we're one nation under God, then we will be one nation gone under."
RONALD REAGAN – 40TH PRESIDENT OF THE UNITED STATES

✝✝✝

At this time in history, we have an opportunity to take ownership of our situation and work toward the basic ideals so brilliantly outlined in the Preamble To The U.S. Constitution by our country's founders: "We the People of the United States, in Order to form a more perfect Union, establish Justice, insure domestic Tranquility, provide for the common defense, promote the general Welfare, and secure the Blessings of Liberty to ourselves and to our Posterity, do ordain and establish this Constitution for the United States of America." The Constitution calls on us to take an active interest in cultivating economic opportunities for all Americans, not just the top 1%, 2% or 5%[11]. Everyone must insist on avoiding aristocracies and the creation of fiefdoms (the state or domain of a feudal lord) in the U.S.—the very structures we rebelled against in the American Revolution. We also think it's important to be mindful of why Congress felt it so important to adopt the phrase "E Pluribus Unum" ("Out of Many, One") and, "In God We Trust" as national mottos.

✝✝✝

"Work is vital to our well–being. Without it, we cannot find genuine fulfillment. God designed us to work."[12]
✝✝✝

In Catholicism, much emphasis is placed on what's called the dignity of work. Under this concept work is both a right and an obligation placed upon us, devised by our Creator. Through work, human beings participate in and help realize God's plan on earth. Work honors the gifts and talents that

God has given each of us. We must work out of regard for others, especially our own family, and also for our society and our country – the whole human family. We are the heirs to the work of generations and at the same time a sharer in building the future of those who will come after us in the succession of history.

Work is a good thing for us - and good for humanity - because through work we not only transform nature, adapting it to our societal needs, but work also helps us to achieve fulfillment as a human being. Pope Benedict XVI's Encyclical Letter on Christmas Day 2005 spoke about these concepts, as follows: "In many cases, poverty results from a violation of the dignity of human work, either because work opportunities are limited (through unemployment or underemployment), or because a low value is put on work and the rights that flow from it, especially the right to a just wage

> **Ca•reer•ology**
>
> *Extreme forms of frugality represent a scarcity mindset and are counter-productive to our country's overall economic situation and, ultimately, our individual success.*

and to the personal security of the worker and his or her family."[13] We pray heartily that our efforts will provide a constructive way to help lift our hurting fellow citizens out of a predisposed mindset of poverty and any circumstance of loss, hopelessness and lack or destitution. We also pray that one day we can capitalize on our renewed strength to more effectively inspire and help our needy brothers and sisters in other countries.

We need to transform ourselves from a scarcity mindset, or believing there is a limit to how abundance can show up in life, back into a prosperity mindset, or believing there is no limit to abundance.[14] Instead of focusing on what is missing or has been lost, we must have faith about what is possible and what our known and unknown opportunities are in terms of creativity, freedom and advancement in our lives. This is the American Dream.

Personal finance gurus regularly express opinions about 'prudent' financial planning activities. Much of this advice has to do with one overriding strategy—being frugal. While cutting spending may pay certain short-term personal dividends, we believe that more emphasis should be placed on other economic factors, such as income improvement. By taking steps to earn more income, you will better achieve your personal objectives and can help others in the process. Indeed, we should be striving to **_earn more, save more, spend more, and give more_**! These actions can help you, your family/community and our country to be a better place to live.

"Ask not what your country can do for you; ask what you can do for your country"
JOHN F. KENNEDY – 35TH PRESIDENT OF THE UNITED STATES

This is not just wishful altruism. The ravages of poverty, unemployment and under-employment affect everyone. We believe we can each do our part to fully respect the dignity of work and the worker. These ideals can be obtained through our hiring and employment practices, through advocacy for widespread gainful employment, excellent working conditions, diversity initiatives, and even by our daily purchase decisions. By working together, we can help create better and broader economic results that will in turn reduce crime, improve physical and mental health, family structures, as well as financial security in our country. We must also have courage and faith in our ability to elect highly-qualified, patriotic and enlightened government officials.

It is through these efforts that the United States will one day be able to enjoy the benefits of an inspired workforce, and serve once again as an exemplary model of widespread social and economic achievement here, and in the eyes of the world. As fully-engaged, motivated individuals, we can build and maintain a much better society within the United States of America!

Jump In and Take Ownership!

CHAPTER 1: THE NEW WORLD OF WORK

Jump In and Take Ownership!

—INTRODUCTION—

The changes we've seen in workplace employment over the last several years rival those of the Industrial Revolution. We are now in another age of transition. Few people are prepared for the impact of this uncertainty and change on their job security, emotional state, resources, and family. No one can count on one employer for a lifetime of job security and benefits. This monumental trend away from implied long-term employment requires each of us to be prepared to make major changes. Most young people have been born into this environment and generally accept it. Each of us, young and old alike, must grow, learn, and perform well at all times. We must become more flexible, adaptable, and visualize ourselves much like a product or service for hire, on a recurring basis. Upon reading this chapter, you will realize the need, value, and importance of change and how developing a new mindset along with good habits can produce tremendous rewards.

NURTURING A COURAGEOUS, CREATIVE AND PRODUCTIVE MINDSET

LAYOFFS, DOWNSIZINGS, CORPORATE RESTRUCTURINGS, AND GLOBALIZATION

Gone are the days of life-long employment with one employer. Think about where your father and grandfathers worked. Chances are they worked for one employer for most of their lives. Compare that to today when workers are changing jobs and careers at a record pace. Everyone in today's working world instinctively knows how employment uncertainty and changes can affect career plans and job security.

✥✥✥

"Progress is impossible without change, and those who cannot change their minds, cannot change anything."

GEORGE BERNARD SHAW – IRISH AUTHOR AND PHILOSOPHER

✥✥✥

In a recent year, 21 million people were downsized or fired in the U.S.[15] Another 25 million left their employer on a voluntary basis during that same year.[16] Numbers like these were unheard of until the 1990's, at least in the white collar workforce. As a result, professional workers are changing employers every 4.6 years.[17] There are several byproducts of these changes. One is the rise of the contingent workforce with almost 1 in 4 employed Americans now working on a contractual, freelance, temporary, and part-time or project basis.[18] That's 25% of the workforce and it's expected to grow to 40%, or 60 million Americans in the next few years.[19]

> ### Ca•reer•ology
> *Despite the growth of online job sites, the majority of people continue to find opportunities via personal and professional networks. No one can do the work for you. You must take charge of your career.*

An excellent book for more information on the contingent workforce is *Free Agent Nation,* by Dan Pink[20] In his book, Pink explains how the employment arena is changing to this type of workforce, which includes self-employed, independent contractors and temporary projects. He describes how free agents view success, including methods of getting work done, and that workers must constantly develop their technological skills. In Careering, we refer to free agents as those who have adopted the mindset of an independent worker and, as such, must be fully responsible for the stewardship of their career.

DIGITAL DIVIDE = DISCONNECTEDNESS

Business relationships were once based on face-to-face interaction. Over the last decade, this has changed as the Internet has helped us expand the reach of our business contacts, networks, marketing platforms and vital information. It has also created a world of frustration, confusion, anxiety, and trepidation, especially for those who have not adapted.

Whatever happened to good, old-fashioned face-to-face meetings? The ease of online connections and reduced amount of direct contact has created an illusion of connectedness—often resulting in nothing more than superficial relationships. In many ways, this new connected/disconnected phenomenon creates unexpected pressure. This is readily apparent to job-seekers subjected to online application processes. If you've been a job applicant in recent years, think about all the times you may have applied online and never received a response … not even a rejection letter or email! That is the time to get out of your home office and do some boots–on–the–ground networking.

"Sow a thought and you reap an action; sow an act and you reap a habit; sow a habit and you reap a character; sow a character and you reap a destiny."
RALPH WALDO EMERSON – AMERICAN ESSAYIST AND POET

Unless key business connections are nurtured and well developed, contacts rarely result in solid job leads, personal introductions, and career success. The good news is with some savvy and persistence, you can connect by phone or in person and stand out. Used correctly, social media can extend your range of initial contacts and serve as a primer.

BUSINESS CYCLES, ECONOMICS, AND THE FUTURE OF JOBS

Historically, career management and job hunting have always been difficult during slow economic times and easier during good economic times. Today, worldwide competition within the New World of Work means more applicants, pursuing the same opportunities during all economic conditions— good, bad, or neutral. Innovations in technology and globalization have erased borders so that competition for work no longer consists of just local or national talent, but also talent from around the world. This strategy is known as outsourcing. This is where companies obtain services from countries with lower labor and production costs to reduce operating expenses. The Internet and globalization permit rapidly developing countries with workers living well below the quality of life in the United States to willingly work for lower wages. This is nothing new and is not rocket science! There will always be someone willing to do similar work, many for less. We must pay close attention to this trend; competition for higher paying jobs and better opportunities will be strong even in good economic times. We may never again see a widespread employees' market. Becoming better prepared through continuous life-long learning, retraining, and by adopting a positive and proactive mental outlook amidst the changes is the future of job survival and advancement.

While these issues facing those pursuing meaningful long-term careers may seem daunting, the good news, thanks be to God, is that new opportunities are created every day. We just need to be alert, especially when significant businesses changes are underway. These changes can create more meaningful jobs, especially for those who treat their careers as if it is a business, designed to adapt to the changing business environment. This requires us to be creative in the way we manage our careers. Taking the anticipatory steps may mean you will enjoy wonderful results.

UNEMPLOYMENT VS. UNDER-EMPLOYMENT

Since 2008, the rate of unemployment has been painfully high. While not all the data is known, everyone needs to understand how difficult it's been for so many people, including those not properly included in the official government numbers.

Based on numerous reports, a reasonable estimate (or what we call 'TruU)' includes between 35 and 40 million Americans hurting from unemployment and under-employment. *This means the official numbers, as of June 2014, were understated by almost 20 million citizens*!

Unemployment and Under-Employment in the United States – 2014		
'Official' Unemployment (U3)	'Official' Unemployment & Under-employment (U6)**	'TruU' An estimate of the actual number of Unemployed and Under-employed***
6.1%	12.1%	24.5%
9,500,000 People*	**18,800,000 People**	**38,000,000 People**
* Plus 3.1 million not counted because their unemployment benefits expired equals 12.6 million - Long-term unemployed not technically included in official statistics. U.S. DOL Bureau of Labor Statistics (June 2014 data). ** U.S. DOL Bureau of Labor Statistics which are supposed to capture the total number of unemployed and under-employed individuals (June 2014 data). *** Estimate of the number of Americans families 'living hand–to–mouth' i.e. unemployed or under-employed. Source: Brookings Institution as reported by CBS News MoneyWatch (April 25, 2014) by Aimee Picchi.		

As of early June 2014, the government's most quoted U3, a statistical unemployment measure, showed almost 6.1% or 9.5 million Americans, out of work. Another measurement, U6 captures what the government calls the under-employed. The U6 data includes the U3 unemployed and also those who are normally full-timers, working part-time due to lack of opportunity and others seeking full-time jobs but who have given up looking for work due to perceived lack of work opportunities. The official U6 measurement included an additional 6% or 9.4 million more workers in distress. By official government measurements, in excess of 18 million citizens were either unemployed or under-employed at that time.[21]

As remarkable as these numbers are, they don't tell the whole story. First, there are many unemployed who aren't included in official statistics, even though some of the numbers are monitored by the U.S. DOL Bureau of

Labor Statistics. Second, while it is true that economic conditions have improved since 2008, evidence suggests that many of the new replacement jobs have come with lower wages,[22] and these are not included in official under-employment statistics. Third, in millions of cases, there is a mismatch between available jobs and workers' skill sets.[23]

THE REST OF THE STORY – DATA THAT IS HARD TO FIND

Below are categories of situations for which little data is available and would help give a more accurate status of the American workforce in the New World of Work.

- Those working multiple part-time jobs and who consider themselves under-employed.
- Those whose incomes and benefits have gone down substantially from pre-Great Recession levels associated with existing and new replacement jobs.
- Those whose skills and education levels are not fully utilized in new replacement jobs.
- Those whose skills and education levels are not adequate or well-suited to new jobs.

Reflection

Even if you have not been impacted by unemployment or under-employment, you probably know someone who has.

1. How might you feel if you had multiple professional degrees, years of experience and were downsized from your employer?
2. How would you feel if you diligently searched for equivalent work but had to settle for multiple part-time jobs just to survive?

A SUCCESSFUL CAREER AND JOB SEARCH STORY

In his own words: The following is a true story of how self-assessment, reflection and proactive networking helped a member of our Career Network Ministry at St. Andrew the Apostle Catholic Church in Apex, North Carolina get started with a new career. He looked outside for guidance and support, and along the way found a path to greater freedom. For purposes of the story, we will refer to him as Jim. All other facts remain unchanged.

Jim Graduates from College – Unsure of His Career Path

A recent graduate with a B.S. degree in biological science from North Carolina State University, Jim was the youngest member of our group and fresh out of college when he started attending our meetings. Like many college graduates, Jim was not sure where he wanted to begin his career. He was a kind, considerate and soft-spoken young person who was struggling with finding a clear career direction. After several months of prayerful contemplation, Jim determined that he wanted to pursue opportunities in the senior and assisted living industry. Unfortunately, Jim had no contacts or experience in the industry and did not know where to start. He credited our Career Network Ministry at St. Andrew in helping him with the career exploration and job search process. He found the Ministry very helpful while he was giving back to others. Presentations provided by guest speakers and open discussions with fellow members helped Jim learn more about ways to explore career options. Upon hearing of his desire and perceived challenges in getting into the senior care industry, members in the group suggested that he enroll in career development classes at a local community college and also consider volunteering at a senior facility. His instructors at the community college reinforced the idea of volunteering.

> ## Ca•reer•ology
>
> *Volunteering in an area where you want to work is a great way to learn more about the type of work/culture and an effective way to develop important contacts. You must take charge of your career.*

Jim Steers Toward the Assisted Living Industry

Jim decided that he would volunteer at least once a week at one or two local senior care facilities along with his part-time job at a local pool supply company. He volunteered in a variety of positions at one senior care facility. He learned about operations and also met many employees. On a separate volunteering project at another senior facility, Jim saw an opportunity to meet with the executive director. He reached out via phone, and they worked out a time Jim could have an informal meeting. He explained how he was exploring opportunities in the senior and assisted living industry and would appreciate any advice or direction the executive director could provide. The executive

7

director appreciated Jim's interest and gave him detailed advice about pursuing opportunities in the industry. Jim thanked him and felt great about making the contact and thrilled that the executive director offered to be available for future assistance.

Volunteering Creates a Great Opportunity

Over the next six months, Jim got to know the activities coordinator at the senior care facility. This was a woman whom Jim would meet each time he volunteered. She got to know him quite well, and realized how passionate he was about the work. Several months later, she was hired into a management position at a new senior facility opening up in the area. Jim contacted her about opportunities at the new facility and she immediately suggested that he complete an application, even though there was no job posted. She enthusiastically encouraged him to apply because of her positive experience in working with him at the previous facility. His application was accepted by the hiring manager and, after some interviews, he got a job in his exact area of interest!

A Model for Success

We believe Jim's actions in exploring and finding a career direction is a model for career success, at any age. He asked for career direction through prayer, proactively obtained valuable first-hand experience and network contacts through volunteering, and was courageous in asking for help and direction from others.

Reflection

Ask yourself how Jim's story can help you find organizations, philosophies, conditions, and environments that represent areas of interest to you and a potential for future job or contract opportunities.

1. How does the New World of Work affect your career choice and industry at this time?
2. What companies or organizations are on your watch list?

MIND, BODY, SPIRIT AND DIGNITY

The New World of Work offers several models for success. To compete, we must be determined and versatile—much like the way top athletes perform in their roles. To win, they exhibit a positive mindset and follow a strict training regimen. Another model of success is performing as if you were an independent consultant, even as you are working as a salaried employee.

One of the most complete guidelines, supporting a successful mindset, are the founding principles of the Young Men's Christian Association or YMCA. The YMCA puts Christian principles into practice by helping members develop a healthy mind, body, and spirit. Developing a professional athlete's attitude and embracing the YMCA principles can make you into a remarkable job seeker and professional worker. You will be able to better clarify, develop and pursue your chosen career goals while maintaining your dignity.

Your dignity is lived out in society by the fulfillment of personal responsibilities. Work is one such essential responsibility which shapes and fulfills human dignity by providing for the needs of one's self and one's family. Work is an essential means by which the goods of the earth and the creative capacities of humans provide for the common good. Human work is the fulfillment of human dignity by engaging in and cooperating with the creative work of God.

GET YOUR CREATIVE JUICES FLOWING

As Americans, we must become more creative and innovative in our work. These are attributes that, surprisingly, have not always been appreciated in corporate America. Innovation is becoming more important to companies as they are forced to compete in the information-driven global economy.

Endless ways exist to develop personal creativity, including brainstorming, mind mapping, and strategizing. We also know through research that developing intellectual capacities can help you become more creative as well. For example, regardless of your professional occupation, the arts, music, nature, and meditation can place your mind in a state that is much more open to creative thought and conscious awareness as to what motivates you. Embracing these types of activities may seem irrelevant to your work life; however, they can help you unlock hidden talents and skills that can improve your work performance and quality of life.

Two books on the subject of creativity and human potential include *How to Think like Leonardo da Vinci,* by Michael J. Gelb,[24] and *Awakening the Giant Within,* by Tony Robbins.[25]

✞✞✞

"Faith is not just a theological principle; it is a mental and environmental muscle."
MARIANNE WILLIAMSON – NY TIMES BESTSELLING AUTHOR

✞✞✞

FAITH, HOPE, AND CHARITY

We now come to the 'attitude-of-gratitude' philosophy on which our faith places so much emphasis. For both authors, this has been of exceptional value throughout our personal and professional challenges. It might have been what supplied air in those times when our oxygen supply seemed so limited. The three heavenly graces of faith, hope, and charity can make all the difference in career management.

Job searching can be one of the least favorite activities a human being can undertake. Prospecting amid challenging job markets and rejections can take a toll on your faith. No one likes rejection. Few like the idea of self-promotion for advancement for new job purposes. However, we believe that by having faith in the gifts God has revealed to us, along with the hope to sustain us during difficult times and the charity to help and love others along the way, we trust that our needs will be met. Amidst all this, are you still being true to yourself? Are these challenges actually a blessing or a gift in disguise?

✞✞✞

"I tell you the truth, whatever you did for one of the least of these brothers of mine, you did for me."
MATTHEW, 25:40

✞✞✞

Reflection

If you are currently experiencing job-loss or potential job-change, ask yourself how you can use the principles of faith, hope, and charity to persevere and forge ahead.

GOOD HABITS PRODUCE GOOD RESULTS!

Top business leaders and professional coaches understand how good habits can make an enormous contribution to your success, while bad habits can hurt, and even kill, your best efforts. Emulating the habits of successful people can be a challenging but effective way to improve your performance.

 Perhaps the most famous book about habits is the blockbuster by Dr. Stephen Covey, *The Seven Habits of Highly Effective People*.[26] Dr. Covey's book outlines how highly effective people do what they do through habit. His approach helps us take ownership in developing productive habits that can translate into a more effective career/life success and balance.

> ## Ca•reer•ology
>
> *I never could have done what I have done without the habits of punctuality, order, and diligence, without the determination to concentrate myself on one subject at a time.* **- Charles Dickens**

✞✞✞

"The subconscious mind – the habitual mind – is over one million times more powerful than the conscious mind."
MAC ANDERSON / JOHN J. MURPHY
AUTHOR, SPEAKER, FOUNDER/CONSULTANT, AUTHOR, SPEAKER

✞✞✞

WHO ARE YOU AND WHAT ARE YOUR HABITS?

Regardless of your current situation, a self-assessment of your habits is an important step in managing your career. This is the process of gathering information about yourself in order to make informed career decisions. Use this time to develop a deeper understanding of yourself and your habits. (Note: Self-assessments of characteristics and preferences are outlined in Chapter 3: Your Career Plan and Personal Brand).

The following reflection exercise can help you qualify and quantify your activities, thoughts and habits with respect to the choices that lead you in both a personal and professional setting.

Reflection

Make a list of all of your major habits. Sort them by productive (good) and non-productive (bad) in two different columns. Be honest with yourself. Start your list of those good habits you are proud of. Next, list the ones you are not proud of—those nagging habits that you've pointed out or know hinder your progress and create obstacles to your success.

Having trouble? Go for a walk by yourself in an environment that you find peaceful like a lake or pond on a beautiful day. Sit down, close your eyes, take a deep breath, and slowly let it out. Allow your mind to open up, and think. Let your creative juices flow.

The following chart provides some examples of good and bad habits.

Identifying Habits	
Example: Good Habits	**Example: Bad Habits**
• I am on time for meetings and in completing important projects.	• I do not always follow through on 'incidental' commitments
• I make sure to build and maintain solid relationships on a professional and personal level on a regular basis.	• I tend to be overly analytical and a control freak most of the time.
• I strive to cherish and maintain my personal family relationships.	• I am so focused on my work that my family is suffering.
• I am a life-long learner, taking advantage of programs that can help me improve.	• I disregard my physical health.

CHANGING HABITS CAN PROPEL YOU

With your list in hand, honor your good habits and begin to address the ones that have not served you so well. Your habits are patterns of behavior that are wired into your subconscious mind, which means that changing them can be like moving a boulder by hand! With awareness comes power. To start this exercise, make minor adjustments at first and work your way forward.

Try not to feel discouraged if you regress, but hold yourself to a high level of personal accountability. A habit, once ingrained through daily practice, will eventually become a new pattern in your psyche, and thus your actions.

Determination and consistency will lead you to success. According to Dr. Maxwell Maltz, a renowned doctor and author of *Psycho–Cybernetics - A Renowned Doctor's Simple, Scientific and Revolutionary Program for Health and Success*: "It takes just twenty-one (21) days to embed new habits."[27]

✝✝✝

"We are what we repeatedly do. Excellence, then, is not an act but a habit."
ARISTOTLE – GREEK PHILOSOPHER AND SCIENTIST

✝✝✝

Reflection

After preparing your "Good and Bad Habits List", show it to an unbiased, trusted friend or confidant for their feedback. Encourage them to speak honestly! Fine-tune your list until it is as accurate as possible. Acknowledge your good habits. Then look for ways to address your bad habits. Hint: This is hard work and you may find yourself regressing at times - you may have to put your ego aside!

1. Remember your friend or confidant will likely see you in ways you cannot see yourself. Keep an open mind and thank them for their help.

2. Refer to your list periodically and be sure to reward yourself for good habits.

God, our Father,

I turn to You, seeking, Your divine help and guidance as I look for suitable employment.

I need Your wisdom to guide my footsteps along the right path and to lead me to find the proper things to say and do in this quest.

I wish to use the gifts and talents You have given me, but I need the opportunity to do so with gainful employment.

Do not abandon me, Dear Father, in this search, but rather grant me this favor I seek so that I may return to You with praise and thanksgiving for Your gracious assistance.

Grant this prayer through Christ, our Lord.

Amen.

Sample Scenario:
Tom is a Baby-Boomer chemical engineer who is panicking after being given a 60-day notice of a job elimination – after 30 years with his company. Below is his plan of action.

Chapter 1: Key Activities Worksheet
Jump In and Take Ownership!

A. Develop self-marketing materials.

What? *Update: LinkedIn profile, resume and*
Initiate conversations with network contacts.

By When? *March 31*

B. Study impact of networking and social media.

What? *Read* 7 Lessons for Better Networking, *by*
Soren Gordhamer, January 18, 2010

By When? *October 1*

C. Read about faith and helping others.

What? *Read James 2:14:17*

By When? *March 1*

D. Make a list of companies/organizations that interest you.

What? *1. Dupont*
2. BASF
3. US EPA
4. Auburn University

By When? *March 15*

Your Turn: *Completing this form will provide you with valuable insights and action steps.*

Chapter 1: Key Activities Worksheet
Jump In and Take Ownership!

A. Develop self-marketing materials.

What? _____
_____

By When? _____

B. Study impact of networking and social media.

What? _____
_____

By When? _____

C. Read about faith and helping others.

What? _____
_____

By When? _____

D. Make a list of companies/organizations that interest you.

What? _____
_____
_____
_____

By When? _____

Download additional templates at www.careeringbook.com

16

Notes & Thoughts

Life Brings Many Twists and Turns

CHAPTER 2: WHY ME? WHY NOT ME?

Life Brings Many Twists and Turns

–INTRODUCTION–

It does not matter who you are—a recent college graduate looking for your first job, a middle-aged worker whose family's livelihood is at risk from job-loss, a former military soldier seeking civilian work, a mother re-entering the workforce, or a senior citizen who cannot afford to retire and must find a new job. Life is a journey full of twists and turns, and this is especially true in the New World of Work. Many seeking sustainable employment today face similar hurdles and, yet often, hidden opportunities. Unanticipated changes, such as job-loss can take a toll on your emotions. Anxiety, fear, and futility can challenge your spirit. You may be asking yourself, "Why me?" questioning your faith and sinking into a negative mindset. The good news: through prayer, faith and a can-do attitude, many job-seekers have risen above their plight and transitioned into a better situation! A few of their stories are captured in this chapter and throughout this book. Never ever forget there is always faith and hope for a brighter future.

BRAVERY AND FAITH CAN PROPEL YOU

✝✝✝

"Be strong and courageous. Do not be terrified; do not be discouraged, for the Lord your God will be with you wherever you go."
JOSHUA, 1:9

✝✝✝

PAUL'S 2ND LAYOFF FROM NORTEL NETWORKS
In his own words: The following is a true story from co-author Paul Dean, describing his most difficult layoff. After being laid off once before, he battled his way back into a new position, only to be laid off yet again. However, this time a terrible new twist impacted the health and well-being of his family.

Laid Off - Then Even Worse News for the Family
It was a tough month for my family and me. First, my company announced at the beginning of the month that a reorganization was coming. Having been part of a downsizing before, this was a code word for layoff.

Next, my wife Barbara called me at work with the results of a tissue biopsy and told me she had breast cancer. I rushed home, we hugged, collapsed to the floor and cried. Our kids, Andrea age five and Chris age four, were at the YMCA at the time and we told them the bad news later that night. They were scared. The next day, everyone at work sensed I was not myself, so I told them about Barbara. They were openly concerned and sympathetic.

A couple of weeks later, my manager dropped by my cubical and asked me to come to an unscheduled meeting. He walked me down the hall to a meeting room and introduced me to a person from the Human Resources (HR) Department. I said hello, shook hands with the HR representative and sat down. No one was smiling, and I felt a huge lump in my throat. After a very long minute, my manager said, "Paul, I'm sorry, but your position in our department has been eliminated." Because I was fully committed to the company and felt many of the people in the company were like family, I was shocked!

20

"In my distress I called upon the Lord; to my God I cried for help. From his temple he heard my voice, and my cry to him reached his ears."
PSALMS, 18:6

I felt like I was stuck in a slow motion, nightmarish dream. I thought to myself—"Is this really happening to us … a cancer diagnosis for my wife, just as I am laid off, again?" I had recovered from the first downsizing and had been rehired by Nortel, but this time, my wife had cancer. "How do I support her emotionally and financially provide for her and the children? My income and benefits have been eliminated! Why her? Why me? Why us?"

Reflection

Regardless of background and circumstances, many people face a difficult time finding and maintaining rewarding work, particularly during tough economic times. If another major life event is happening at the same time, as was the case with Paul, it's even harder. You will feel one or more emotions—anxiety, fear, discouragement, hurt and perhaps even depression, bitterness and anger. These feelings are not unusual, especially with job-loss and consequent family issues, and it's normal to feel this way, at least for a temporary period.

1. How does Paul's story illustrate one of the main worries that comes up with a sudden job-loss? How can you prepare for this in the future? How can you support your partner or be supported if this happens in your family?

2. When challenges happen to you, do you find that you ask yourself, "Why did this happen to me?" Do you see yourself as a victim? Do you see the opportunity behind the challenge?

> ### Ca•reer•ology
> *In the New World of Work, you are not alone! With ever-changing social-economics, jobs and careers constantly change and evolve. Be sure to stay current and well-networked. Always remember: When one door closes, another one opens.*

DEPRESSED AND CONFUSED – NOW WHAT?

A check up from the neck up! Negative emotions can become destructive over time and can prevent you from moving on. It's normal to need time to grieve, reflect and heal following job-loss. Developing a positive mental attitude and taking initial steps towards a new goal will lead you to recovery and success. Be sure to have created and then utilize your support system of trusted friends, family, and colleagues. Do not isolate yourself!

 A great book on the subject of overcoming negativity is called *Feeling Good – The New Mood Therapy,* by David D. Burns, M.D.[28] Dr. Burns covers a wide range of issues around negativity and depression, including root causes of the problems and drug-free behavioral change recommendations for improvement. Dr. Burns does not recommend any self-help book as a substitute for professional therapy, and we believe anyone experiencing prolonged or clinical depression, should seek professional help.

Change is normal, and you are not alone if you are being forced into the job transition process. Like millions of people, we too have experienced—and continue to experience—career challenges, including unexpected job losses. We've worked hard to deal with our emotions by responding to the challenges and seeking positive solutions.

✞✞✞

"To overcome any challenge and create transformational results in sales and business, you need to get your mind right and develop a prosperity mindset that is geared and programmed to transcend any obstacle."
WELDON LONG – NY TIMES BESTSELLING AUTHOR

✞✞✞

THE GOOD, THE BAD, YOUR FOCUS

Most of the new jobs or opportunities we've found throughout the years have been more rewarding than many of those lost. This may be God's way of redirecting us toward our true calling. We sincerely believe, by accepting the challenges, you may be able to make a better life for yourself and your loved ones.

We must all learn to focus better! Proper focus is an often untapped, yet incredibly powerful tool. Your mind and actions can make a bad situation worse or a good situation better. For example, in job search groups, some people focus on the same negatives – "It's a poor economy" or "I'm too old" are common complaints. This type of focus is unproductive and saps positive energy from you and those around you. Similar to throwing gasoline on a fire, recurring negative talk makes the problem bigger and can stifle a person's opportunities for growth.

Conversely, positive thoughts and positive reinforcement from others can increase your energy level and help you succeed. Is this too good to be true? No! Numerous examples of success have been reported that support the value of positive thoughts and actions, by simply capitalizing on your natural human energy.[29]

✥✥✥

"Your work is not your worth."
DAVID M. BURNS, M.D. – PROFESSOR EMERITUS, STANFORD/AUTHOR

✥✥✥

SELF-WORTH AND 'JOB'

Numerous studies show that many professional workers' value of self is determined by their jobs, at least when measured by job-loss.[30] This is especially true for Baby Boomers. In addition, we know that "What do you do?" is often the first question asked at both business meetings and social functions. The truth is that while your career may be important in your lives, it should not be as important as other aspects of your life. How do you put your work into proper perspective? This requires you to take a different point of view and the answer usually depends on what you value. There is no simple answer to this question, except how you view yourself, your life's journey, and how you deal with the situation. For example, if you make security and financial gain the driving force of your choices, you will have a harder time managing an unforeseen lay-off or discharge, especially if you had counted on your job for retirement, the purchase of a home, or that planned dream vacation. If you see yourself as a God-centered individual, made in the image and wholeness of God, and that God has a plan, your reaction may be different than that of someone who does not have faith. Your perspective may determine your effectiveness in managing your career.

It's clear that your work does not define your human and spiritual value. Your significance or personal worth is not defined by your employer, or your title. Losing a job or a contract does not negate your value as a human being with much to contribute. Think of this change as an opportunity to help you figure out where you truthfully need to be.

Having exceptional work experience and advanced skills will give you an edge. These improve your employability, marketability and earning potential but should not lock you into your current job. In fact, this is where you may realize that you are free to choose where you want to be and do what will make you feel valued and part of a greater plan.

STORIES OF CAREER AND LIFE COURAGE
In their own words: The following are true stories about the career/life successes and failures of a few other members of our Career Network Ministry at St. Andrew the Apostle Catholic Church.

Sandra's Story - Life Interrupted

From a very early age, the driving force in my life was growth and contribution. My focus was about learning and being in the middle of new and exciting experiences. As a result, I've lived a life full of variety, excitement, opportunity, fun, dreams fulfilled, and, as you may guess, a level of uncertainty that comes with living life according to your own beat and not someone else's.

I was born in Colombia, South America, and I immigrated to the United States at the age of nine. With a love of languages, I learned English and became the unofficial interpreter for new kids arriving. I have always felt a strong connection to God and had an innate awareness of the spiritual context of my life in helping others through my own experiences. I felt that life was open to me, and I never worried about my future or how I would get there.

Embarking on a Diverse Life

In college, I majored in French and spent my last semester as an exchange student in Avignon, France. This led to my decision to become an international flight attendant and language speaker from the age of 21 until 38 years old. At age 38, I faced a defining point in my life, one in which God decided to intervene and forge a new path for my life! Those seventeen years served as stepping stones to many interests and irreplaceable life experiences. Living in Manhattan for much of the period, I became a voice-over performer, a commercial print-model and Screen Actors Guild (SAG) actor. I got married, learned Italian and, unfortunately, got divorced five years later. I had a child as a single mother, joined the Air Force Reserve as a public affairs specialist and journalist. I went on to receive an MBA and travelled the world, oftentimes enjoying a lifestyle usually associated with wealth and abundance. I was living life and had plans to continue travelling forever!

Life Takes a Bad Turn

Then God interrupted my course. During one of my flights in 2000, I suffered a work injury that left me with multiple cervical and lumbar hernias that continuously challenged me for the next seven years. After five reoccurring injuries, in 2005, I was left unable to walk, stand, and function without great discomfort and pain. I spent two years on disability, depleted my 401K, gave up my health insurance and life insurance, and lost all my credit. I had every creditor calling me for payments that I could not make and inevitably had my car repossessed. I was approved for a total disc replacement to which I opted out. I eventually decided to quit after 17 years even bearing in mind that I had only three years remaining until retirement. I was physically unable to work or support myself or child and dependent on my family for my livelihood. That was 2007.

God Intervenes and Redirects Sandra

While this situation was physical and charged with emotional challenges, this, in my interpretation, was a message from God to redirect my purpose. Being 'connected' to my spiritual essence, I saw this as an invitation and opportunity for emotional growth and personal preparation. Had this not happened five years in a row, I would not have interpreted it as God directing me away from continuing as a flight attendant. I was not going where I needed to be in order to do what I came here to create and deliver. It took the next eight years of fortitude, belief, faith, hope, prayer, education, training and experience for me to claim my purpose and launch my own business. In the process of defining my gifts and forging my career as a personal development coach and spiritual awakening catalyst, I made sacrifices to my economic stability and physical comfort. Rather than selling out to a company for a stable paycheck, I chose to remain free and organic, while uncovering my message and vision.

God's Plan

Knowing my calling as a difference-maker and coach for a concept called 'awakened personal empowerment', I crafted my vision to help youth and families transform from their limited perceptions as individuals to mission-minded difference-makers in this lifetime. Because of my injury, I also became privy to some technological advances that I believe helped the body to heal itself naturally, and as a result, I was able to regain my ability to function physically without surgery or drugs. I am living testament to these blessings and now a messenger to help others as I help the environment and planet in the process.

Accepting the Truth

It has not been easy, but I have been true to my internal light. I have not sacrificed my being for the comfort of money and stability. I have pushed myself to uphold my values, beliefs, our world and our inclination for comfort and convenience. I have embraced the Catholic Foundation and its teachings through my volunteering as a middle school youth catechist at Saint Andrew the Apostle Catholic Church. I now understand what our precepts are and how we can use our uniquely inspired gifts to touch the world and to inspire a change that will touch those that cross our paths. In this world of confrontation, it is my belief that, as Christians, we must be fundamentally centered on what scripture says and what the Catholic social teaching represents in order to serve and help ourselves while also helping and serving others. This means being true to our innate calling, no matter the price, and heeding God's direction when something like an accident, a job-loss, or a health challenge crosses our path. Oftentimes we ask God for solutions and help, and when He answers, we fail to see or understand the bigger meaning.

"May you be blessed with understanding when something that you want or are pursuing does not come your way. Be bold, faithful and vigilant because God has a plan!"
SANDRA BUENO

Reflection

1. How can Sandra's story help you define your direction and appreciate the life challenges you've experienced?

2. If you are being faced with physical or economic challenges, how can your perspective help you define your focus and path?

3. Earnestly ask God to lead you in the path you were born to live. Listen and be open to His response. Be courageous to follow your inner calling to act.

"Genuine faith is not just speculative belief – it creates a runway for success in your life and career."
DANA AND PAUL

In their own words: Mac and Pam – Both with Professional Degrees, Both Suddenly out of Work, and a Family of Four.

Authors' Note: Mac and Pam's story illustrates a common situation in which the New World of Work puts pressures on families to adapt and make difficult decisions to support and raise a family. This is a great example of how people like Pam and Mac had to learn how to withstand a relocation, job search, and career transition. They learned the importance of building a solid network in helping to manage their careers.

Ca•reer•ology

Life can be a journey towards enlightenment. Sometimes our reasons for being here are not aligned with our purpose for living and working. Reflect deeply on your life and work and try answering the big question about why you are on Earth.

A Move to North Carolina – Hoping for Stability

In 2002, after 20 years with a microchip company in Ohio, I learned that my company was closing its Ohio location and that my only option with them was to transfer my family to a facility in North Carolina where I would work as a product and test engineering manager. My husband Mac resigned his position as manager of consulting services at the University of Findlay (Ohio) Environmental Resource Training Center to work as a contract instructor, servicing clients of the same organization throughout the U.S. Unfortunately, in 2004, his contract was not renewed, and he was instantly jobless. Then, not long after his dismissal, I was told that my position was changing again and being moved to California. With a daughter who would soon be a senior in high school, in our eyes moving to California was not a viable option for our family. We found ourselves both out of work at the same time.

Embracing Change

I was devastated about leaving my job. I had survived at least at a half dozen layoffs during the time I was with the company. The job was a big part of my life, both professionally and socially, not to mention it was the only paycheck coming into our family for a time. While the company did provide some professional assistance and severance, I was still angry and bitter. I cried, I prayed and I felt betrayed by the place that I had given so much to. While all these emotional challenges were going on, we also had to deal with financial issues, including getting health insurance and slashing every extraneous expense we could think of to stay afloat. Meantime, Mac had tried to start his own business, but with all his connections in Ohio and our immediate need for income, he switched gears and began looking for traditional work. He began to attend local networking groups in his profession and also at the St. Andrews Career Network Ministry at our church.

Pam Explores a Career Transition

It had been years since I had to find and win employment. At the same time, I was trying to determine if I should stay in the microchip business or try something new. Since I had not really discovered my passion in my career life, I spent some time attempting to do so. There was a lot of soul searching and pondering over what I enjoyed and what I didn't. I enrolled in classes at the community college to assist in the discovery process. I decided to leave the microchip industry behind and focus my efforts on moving into the medical devices, which I perceived would be more stable. With more recent experience in product development, testing, quality and compliance, I sculpted my resume with a focus on my skill sets and experience directly transferrable to the medical device industry.

28

How Networking Helped Pam

Before I was out of work, I did not network. The networking scene was very difficult for me. I don't gather energy from other people like my husband does. The thought of going to networking events left me depressed. Knowing it was the primary path out of the situation; I motivated myself, and got on with it. I suppose as time went on, I became better at it, but networking is still way out of my comfort zone. I researched the local networking functions and meetings that focused on medical devices, quality and even project management.

At first, I was very forceful in my networking efforts. I was desperate, and I am certain it showed through in my actions. It didn't take me long to realize that I needed to behave like it was a social event and not a 'witch hunt' for a job (even though it was in my mind). Many times, Mac and I would attend networking functions together and grab a cup of coffee afterward to discuss the situation. It was the closest we got to a date out in months!

Volunteering Leads to Part-Time Work

We did take time out from the job hunt to volunteer intermittently. This was great because it ended up being an informal method of networking without actually feeling like we're networking. The situation was more relaxed and we're focused on helping others and not totally worrying about a job. We continually networked while volunteering and attended our daughter's volleyball games, finding ways to help others and share with them our situation.

Our two daughters were both very supportive during our job hunt and occasionally offered up jobs they saw online. Quite by accident, the volleyball games did land Mac a part-time job with a local tree trimming service. Mac and the coach's husband got into a conversation at one of the girl's games. One thing led to another, and before we knew it, he was working part-time trimming trees and landscaping (which he did have some experience doing). We were forever thankful for that opportunity.

Fighting Depression

Several months had gone by, and the whole job hunting thing was getting very depressing. One of us really needed a long term, full-time job in our area of expertise. There were a lot of sleepless nights and the uncertainty of everything was unnerving. Continual prayer and trust in God were prominent during this period. Finally, after a couple of months of active networking and staying focused on our primary goals, we both gathered some decent leads.

Pam Targets Companies and Follows-Up

I utilized introductions from my networking leads for entry into various companies with openings in my area of interest and experience. A formal resume and cover letter crafted specifically for each open position was always my first step. This was followed up with more documentation as to why I was 'the person for the job'. I researched the companies, learning about their products, their history and open positions. I initiated email and phone contact to further express my interest. I was successful in getting interviews at several companies, using this approach. After my interviews, I provided needs/contribution summaries to the hiring manager, showcasing how I could contribute in the areas where the company needed assistance, even though my previous job was in another industry.

Pam's Transition into a New Industry

I was ultimately rewarded with two job offers and chose to go with a small start-up in the medical device arena. While I did take a position and pay cut to move across industries, my new employer quickly realized my abilities, and I was promoted twice in just a few years, working nearer the level that I had been in my previous company. It was small, and we all wore many hats, but everyone there really worked as a team.

Mac's Job Lead from Pam's Network

Not long after I joined the start-up company, Mac landed a new position as well. An introduction into a local safety group meeting that came from the husband of a woman I met at a class during my job hunt, provided a job lead from three members of that safety group. It was a position very similar to his work in Ohio. He was ecstatic because it aligned with his passion, and he was perfect for the job.

Networking Never Ends for Pam

I realized that, even though I landed this first job in the start-up medical device company, there was another company I liked but at the time they did not have an open position. Through continuous networking, I was able to make contact with a certain individual inside the company. I introduced myself, forwarded my resume and started my sales pitch. They agreed to meet with me. I rehearsed what I would say over and over. The day finally came and I showcased my skills and experience, focusing on how I could assist the company in achieving their goals.

While it appeared that I was received favorably, the company was not quite ready to bring on another employee. I had received a job offer from another local (very large) company under a contract, but I was really interested in going with the start-up. I let them know my situation, but the timing just wasn't right. I told them I needed to take the contract position to help support my family, but that I was very much interested in working with them and vowed to keep in touch.

> ## Ca • reer • ology
> *No one grows without challenges, and oftentimes unexpected outcomes are just a way to break you out of your comfort zone.*

Three months later, while on a business trip, I saw the gentlemen from my 'perfect company' in the Atlanta airport. I walked down to the next gate where they were camped out. "Hey, how's it going? Fancy meeting you guys here." They chimed back, "Great, how are you? What brings you to Atlanta?" It was comforting that they remembered me. We had a nice catch-up conversation, and I decided then that I would stay in touch.

Pam's Proactive Networking Pays Off

A few months later, I crafted an email to the CEO, letting him know I was still interested in working there and inquired about the status of the company. He replied, "Let's talk." Not long after, I was offered a position. I have been with the company for 18 months now, working in quality assurance and compliance. Where there's a will, there's a way, and I know that I must continue to be proactive in managing my career and continue to network my way into new opportunities because jobs and industries are continually changing.

Reflection

Change can be stressful, especially during temporary periods of real or perceived failures, rather than lessons toward improvement. As illustrated in

31

these stories, even the most accomplished people experience setbacks or failures, sometimes on multiple occasions.

1. Looking back, how have your setbacks or failures helped you to grow and become better?

2. When experiencing a loss or setback, do you reach out and share and discuss your feelings with your spouse?

An excellent resource for career inspiration, failure and success stories is the book, *Steve Jobs,* by Walter Isaacson.[31]   Steve Jobs blazed a path for himself and, in so doing, helped to connect the world.

ATTITUDE COUNTS!
POSITIVE IS GOOD. NEGATIVE IS BAD – PERIOD !

For many years, experts have suspected that positive attitudes pay dividends. Research has now proven that an overall positive outlook or 'happiness' generally results in less unemployment, more productivity and a healthier and longer life.[32]   Obviously, it's hard to always have a positive attitude, especially during difficult times, such as a job loss.

Positive thinking is tied very closely to the theological virtue of hope. Pope Benedict XVI, in his second encyclical letter, Spe Salvi (Saved by Hope), emphasizes the indispensability of hope for those who encounter suffering of whatever depth: "The present, even if it is arduous, can be lived and accepted if it leads towards a goal, if we can be sure of this goal, and if this goal is great enough to justify the effort of the journey" (Spe Salvi 1).[33] Hope enables us to look past or beyond the negative feelings of a job loss, but it also inspires and refocuses our actions in a new direction.

"Ability is what you're capable of doing. Motivation determines what you do. Attitude determines how well you do it."
LOU HOLTZ, AMERICAN FOOTBALL PLAYER, COACH, AND ANALYST

The duration and magnitude of any negative feelings is important to track. Why draw a distinction between normal emotional grief from illness, divorce, job-loss or death and chronic negativity? This is critical to understand because temporary grief is normal and healthy, based on real events, whereas chronic negativity represents imaginary thoughts about problems in the future. Philosopher P.D. Ouspensky remarked, "Of many people, it is possible to say that all their lives are regulated and controlled, and in the end ruined, by negative emotions". [34] Evidence suggests that extreme cases of chronic negativity may be a psychological condition, possibly unavoidable for some people.

If you continue to express and manifest negative thoughts about everything, then you may be sick. For more information about pervasive negativity, see the article by Cloe Madanes called *14 Habits of Miserable People*.[35]

Many who have just lost their jobs undergo a relentless battle with negative emotions. Exhausted savings, creditors, an unsupportive spouse and other forces take a toll. In some cases, people are able to rise above this situation by counting their blessings and taking a perspective that others may have it worse—much worse. Although this realization provides no permanent remedy, it can lessen a person's negative outlook. We encourage everyone to devote some time to volunteering to help others who are less fortunate. Working on being positive and taking action will lead you back to success.

Sarah Lewis, a chartered organizational psychologist and author, argues that when people are positive, it can lead to opportunities because they are more engaged and resilient.[36] Positivity is being able to have the end-in-sight, even if there is only darkness around you. The Bible teaches us to count our blessings and be thankful for what we have and the beautiful world God has created. It's so much more fun and healthy being positive. Finding techniques to be positive and expressing your upbeat viewpoint will energize you and everyone you encounter.

The article by Amy Morin, *Positive Thinking Isn't A Substitute For Positive Action*,[37] tells us that by combining positive thinking with positive action will help you get beneficial results.

Reflection

To help with positivity, focus on the following:

1. Purge all negative sentiments you have of yourself.
2. Think about developing mental pictures of pleasant thoughts. List positive actions you can take in light of your current situation.
3. Keep a list of things that you are grateful for each day.

DO YOUR BEST AND FORGET THE REST

The title of the song *You're Only Human,* by Billy Joel says it all.[38] We are, in fact, only human—it's ok to make mistakes—that's how we learn. When addressing the issues you've identified for improvement, focus on what you can control and let go of the things you cannot. This is a major lesson for you to learn in both your personal and professional life. You can only control the inputs, not the outputs.

> ## Ca•reer•ology
> *If you've earnestly given it your best, then let God do the rest!*

This is how St. Joseph responded to God's request. He acted obediently, without any guarantee or control over his success. Joseph had no advance knowledge about what outcomes he would experience. He simply exhibited faith and trust in God and just look at the miracles that occurred.

Another important element in doing your best has to do with your everyday interactions at work and home. It's the little things that often get in the way. They prevent us from becoming a better parent, husband, wife and friend. Think about the people you work with. Who do you enjoy spending time with? What does your attitude, demeanor, disposition, and outlook bring to the relationship? Are you a positive contributor, who repeatedly has something good to share, or are you a negative contributor, who rarely smiles and provides nothing but complaints?

Becoming a role model and refraining from being dragged into the negative camps will work wonders for your soul. Be positive and authentic. Praise others, and you will be performing a great service for your family, co-workers and yourself. Remember the little things, like saying Thank You when it is deserved. Those two words make for a much better day for yourself and those you meet.

The table on the next page provides some tools and practices you can use to help promote a better work/life balance that support personal character development and relations. Set aside time each day for one or more of these activities.

34

Powerful Tools for Living and Working	
• Humor/Fun	• Prayer
• Gratitude	• Music
• Love	• Volunteering
• Dreaming	• Meditation
• Simplification	• Praise
• Nature	• Forgiveness
• Exercise	• Family Activities/Fun

Decide what activities best fit your interests best and build them into your regular schedule. Some activities may be undertaken alone while others can and should include friends and family. By taking time for your personal interests outside of work, you should find that your life, relationships and career will benefit.

Heavenly Father,

Help me to forget the negative things and feelings

I have from my job layoff.

Give me strength not to dwell on mistakes and failures

from my last year.

God, I believe that You will give me the grace and

strength to adapt to the rapidly changing work

environment and find new career opportunities.

I believe that You will make rivers and streams in

the wilderness and deserted places in my life.

In Jesus' Name I pray.

Amen

✝✝✝

Sample Scenario:
Bill is a discouraged, 55 year-old laid-off Operations Manager in the auto industry – out of work for 3 years. Below is his plan of action.

Chapter 2 Key Activities Worksheet
Life Brings Many Twists and Turns

A. Evaluate the Consequences of Prolonged Negative Emotions vs. a Positive-Minded Approach.

What? *Brainstorm and list positive actions I can take based on my current situation*

By When? *Next week*

B. Seek Professional Career Guidance from a Highly Trained Specialist.

What? *Ask for referrals from friends, family and former colleagues.*

By When? *October 1*

C. Read About the failures and success of highly successful people.

What? *Henry Ford, Abraham Lincoln, and Thomas Edison on Wikipedia*

By When? *November 1*

D. Volunteer to help start a Career Ministry at your church.

What? *Recruit 1 or 2 fellow volunteers*

By When? *October 15*

Your Turn: *Completing this form will provide you with valuable insights and action steps.*

Chapter 2 Key Activities Worksheet
Life Brings Many Twists and Turns

A. Evaluate the Consequences of Prolonged Negative Emotions vs. a Positive-Minded Approach.

What? _____

_____

By When? _____

B. Seek Professional Career Guidance from a Highly Trained Specialist.

What? _____

_____

By When? _____

C. Read About the failures and success of highly successful people.

What? _____

_____

By When? _____

D. Volunteer to help start a Career Ministry at your church.

What? _____

_____

By When? _____

Download additional templates at www.careeringbook.com

Notes & Thoughts

Who Am I And How Am I Perceived?

CHAPTER 3: YOUR CAREER PLAN AND PERSONAL BRAND

Who am I and How am I Perceived?

–INTRODUCTION–

Without an inspiring plan, life and work can be difficult and tedious. Even with a plan, you must adapt and be willing to accept change. Do you have a career plan? In the New World of Work, you must be creative and entrepreneurial. That could mean running your own business or consulting practice temporarily or permanently. As you pursue traditional employment, you must take ownership of your career—and adopt a free agent's mindset. In adopting this mindset, you will gain opportunities by branding your professional reputation—and then marketing your brand to meet individual and organizational needs. This will require you to step out of your comfort zone. Learning to adapt, to find balance, peace, and satisfaction, though not easy, can help you not only to survive, but thrive under the circumstances. Upon reading this chapter, you will learn how to anticipate and appreciate change, embrace networking, skill-building, and the importance of actively managing your career and personal brand.

REFLECTION, INTENTION, AND EFFORT BRING US CLOSER TO OUR DEEPEST DESIRES

✝✝✝

"One of the most positive transitions you can make is from viewing your work as a job to viewing it as a calling."
MARIANNE WILLIAMSON, - NY TIMES BESTSELLING AUTHOR

✝✝✝

YOUR LIFE'S WORK: HISTORY IN THE MAKING

Change. Consider that just a century ago an industrial revolution transformed our country from a farming society to a heavily-industrialized nation. Before then, making buggy whips was a widespread occupation! Imagine the fear and frustration that millions of workers must have felt in this elimination of long-standing jobs, and at the same time, the mixed emotions that many must have experienced when leaving the family farm in favor of factory work.

In recent years, we have experienced another revolution from globalization, the Internet and Great Recession that changed most jobs and many companies. It's hard to predict the rise or fall of any particular company, and sometimes these changes can be brutal. Just look at those who are now employed by corporations, such as Google, Microsoft, Facebook vs. Enron and Nortel Networks, where mass lay-offs affected the lives of thousands, almost overnight.

RESEARCH PAYS OFF

It's important to be aware of changes going on within your environment. Regardless of whether you are actively working or temporarily out-of-work, you must stay informed. You must research and find up-to-date information about your existing or desired occupations.

"Smell the cheese often so you know when it is getting old."
SPENCER JOHNSON – BESTSELLING AUTHOR "WHO MOVED MY CHEESE?"

✝✝✝

As you research the trends of industries and companies, including your own, you will obtain a clearer perspective on where your career is headed.

This will take time, but your efforts will help you to make more informed decisions. While you may not be able to accurately forecast the future standing of any company or their long-term longevity, you can better position yourself for success by staying informed. Research will help you identify what the near-term and long-term prospects look like for the type of work you desire. You will be able to determine whether the field is expanding or shrinking.

Finally, by researching organizations, including corporate performance results, company culture and trends, you may become aware of changes before they occur. In some cases, you may even find a way to avoid the layoff bullet by making a job change ahead of time!

ADAPTING TO THE NEW WORLD OF WORK

We must embrace and accept change to survive and thrive in the rapidly changing New World of Work. Today's changes stem from technological advances, globalization, and a persistent effort by employers to achieve more output with fewer workers or 'do more with less'. To adapt, we must meet or exceed expectations and remain open-minded to unexpected changes and new opportunities. Additional trends include:

- Substantial movement by employers toward the Contingent Workforce comprised of independent contractors, part-time and temporary positions;
- Multiple job changes, employment arrangements and complete career changes
- An emphasis on skills, certifications, and accomplishments and competencies in hiring decisions

The U.S. Government's Occupational Outlook and O*Net are two resources that provide current employment information. They can be found at www.bls.gov/ooh/ or www.onetonline.org. Additionally, state governments, as well as universities and colleges, also produce career data. Local employment agencies have updated data on employment and employers.

Note: Your research about careers and jobs should include financial rewards, such as pay, benefits, incentives, and bonus information, so that you can make informed decisions about the companies you are considering.

✛✛✛

"I tell you the truth, if you have faith as small as a mustard seed, you can say to this mountain, 'Move from here to there' and it will move. Nothing will be impossible for you."
MATTHEW, 17:20

✛✛✛

DANA TURNS LEMONS INTO LEMONADE WITH A CAREER CHANGE

In his own words: Below is a true story from co-author Dana Gower, describing how an unexpected downsizing ultimately led to a new career and an opportunity to help people in job transition.

Shame and Embarrassment

In 1999, I was working as a director of human resources within a unit of a Fortune 500 company when I was called into my boss's office—on Easter Monday. I had 17 years with the company, notable accomplishments, and was well-respected.

My boss had a serious look on his face when he asked me to sit down. His wife had recently died of cancer, so I really didn't know what was on his mind. He looked at me and told me that he had decided to terminate my job. "We like you, but…" is all he said—nothing else. I was floored. My first thought was "Oh no, my youngest kids, Reid and Hannah, are only ages 5 and 3, and my wife is a full-time stay-at-home mom. What do I tell her and my older kids—Erin, Katie, and Danielle? What if I have trouble finding a new job?" I felt shame and embarrassment. For the first time in my life, I was also nervous about the possibility of not earning a paycheck.

> **Ca•reer•ology**
> *The more you understand yourself, the better you will be able to function, and the more effective you will become in managing your career.*

44

Taking the Bull by the Horns

While I had enjoyed my time in corporate America, being on a fixed salary and weathering the politics of a major company had grown old. The massive number of downsizings I helped implement in these last few years had taken its toll on me. Armed with degrees in finance and a background in human relations and employee benefits, I decided to transition to a career as a financial and estate planner. I knew from my research that I would have unlimited income opportunities in a growing industry. I set up interviews and accepted a job with a great financial organization after passing the necessary regulatory exams. I then developed a marketing plan and set out to obtain clients, which I did and was very successful. In fact, in my first year, I made more money than I did in my final year in my corporate job! From there, along with another Fortune 500 refugee colleague of mine, I decided to focus on serving people undergoing job transition. Together we produced a seminar that went national throughout outplacement agencies across the U.S. and a book to go along with it—*The Career and Financial PowerBook*. Ultimately, we even sold the rights to the seminar to the financial services giant we were working for!

Reflection

We hope Dana's story will inspire others to consider all career possibilities. Had Dana not been terminated from his job, he would not have had the opportunity to produce and launch a successful nationwide seminar that has helped so many clients and others undergoing job transition.

1. How can your past trials and tribulations be useful in helping others?
2. Remember always: When one door closes, another one opens. Where can you see this in your past, present and future?

The agony of Jesus in the Garden at Gethsemane points the way for us to understand the redemptive value of the suffering we experience in our own lives. In doing His Father's will, Jesus drinks the cup—undergoes His Passion—for our salvation. With God's grace, we too must seek His will always, even if it causes us pain and suffering.

KNOW YOURSELF AND EXPAND YOUR VISION

A proper self-assessment includes a look at hard skills, such as computer competencies, industry knowledge, and specific work task skills, along with soft skills, such as values, interests, and relationship abilities. If you have not completed any self-assessments, try some.

Take inventory of your career assets, such as writing, speaking, technical, financial, personality, and your ability to function under stress. This will help you to understand what you are good at doing. If this sounds overwhelming, start with just one or two assessments and build from there. Taking self-assessments is required in order to truly dig into self. The most popular self-assessments include:[39]

- **Myers Briggs Type Indicator (MBTI)** – A questionnaire that measures psychological characteristics and preferences in how people perceive the world and make decisions.
- **StrengthsFinder** – An assessment tool and philosophy that outlines a person's strengths, with emphasis on building on those strengths, rather than on weaknesses.
- **DISC** – A behavior assessment tool based upon four different personality traits: dominance, inducement, submission, and compliance.
- **Insights Discovery** – Using color categories, tool helps a person better understand his/her personality and communication ability, as well as those of others.
- **Page Work Behavior Inventory** – Helps leaders and professionals better understand work style, influencing/selling style, personality characteristics, emotional intelligence, and behavioral potential.
- **Career Lift Off Interest Inventory** – A tool to help students and experienced workers in choosing a career path that is rewarding, meaningful, and enjoyable.
- **Seven Stories Exercise** – A plan of action, consisting of writing seven stories about one's life from childhood to present to better understand individual patterns and the elements to look for in an enjoyable career.

- **Type Verifier** – A measurement of personality types that can help with understanding a career and life from a 'best fit' based upon preferences.
- **SkillScan** – A self-directed skills assessment tool that features a comprehensive profile of transferable skills and preferences.
- **The Self-Directed Search (SDS)** – A career interest test that asks questions about aspirations, activities, skills, and interests; helps match with occupations.

Utilizing these tools may help you to develop a better understanding of what's called your 'Emotional Intelligence'. Two leading researchers on this subject, Peter Salovey and John D. Mayer, define emotional intelligence as "the ability to monitor one's own and others' feelings and emotions, to discriminate among them and to use this information to guide one's thinking and actions".[40] Having effective emotional intelligence can be more important than IQ in life and career success. Emotional intelligence can help you monitor and manage around different personalities, work cultures, and circumstances.

> **Ca•reer•ology**
> *If you have a difficulty interpreting assessments by yourself, seek advice from a mentor, trusted friend or a professional career coach.*

Career interest surveys can serve as excellent planning tools, regardless of the stage of your career. We often think of these tools as being applicable only to recent high school or college graduates. However, given the ever-changing nature of the work world, knowing an up-to-date status of your interests and abilities can help you pinpoint your desired next step for a job or maybe alternative employment, such as starting your own business.

Reflection

Parenting is a good test of utilizing emotional intelligence, and the workplace at times can be like grade school!

1. What did you experience and how did emotional intelligence come into play while you were raising your children?
2. Read the book, *Coping With Difficult People,* by Robert M. Bramson, PhD[41]. This is like a user's manual for interaction.

ACCURATE ASSESSMENTS PAY OFF

In his own words: Following is a description of how prior performance reviews helped Paul in his evolving career journey.

A Brand New Point of View

I hated performance reviews! My manager at Nortel did not like doing them any more than I did. Every year it seemed like Human Resources (HR) would rename the process in an effort that I believed was designed to make 'them' (the HR Department) justify their existence and 'us' (the employees) feel valued. Our process was called Management for Achievement (MFA).

During the review and following a formalized scripted form, my manager would review my job duties, and together we would discuss and document my strengths and weaknesses and put together a plan for my continuous improvement. Once we completed the form, he filed a copy with HR, and I received a copy for my records. At the time, I found the reviews awkward and a complete waste of time. But I was wrong! Only after my layoff did I realize these MFA assessments turned out to be critical in helping me initiate an overall career self-assessment. I did not appreciate any of the feedback at the time, but in reality, this tool helped me to develop my resume and appreciate the importance of career planning after I was laid off.

Reflection

When experiencing an unexpected job loss, part of our self-esteem and sense of purpose is also lost. This can be linked to studies, showing that our lives and our identification are centered on our occupation. Our self-worth drives us to identify with what we do, rather than who we are as individuals. Suddenly, wham! Your job ends, and your identity is lost. Consider the following:

1. Where do you go from here? How do you start again? What personal attributes, talents, gifts and experiences do you have that can help you recreate yourself?

2. How can you objectively assess yourself in figuring what talents make you unique? Who can you illicit to help you figure it out? What negative thoughts do you need to purge to allow yourself to see and not undervalue your capacities?

Fortunately for Paul, he had prior performance reviews that helped him assess his skills and begin to explore his career options.

"Constant change and uncertainty make any traditional career strategy ineffective...Competition for opportunity is fierce."

REID HOFFMAN – CO-FOUNDER OF LINKEDIN

BEN CASNOCHA – WRITER, ENTREPRENEUR

KNOW YOUR TRANSFERABLE SKILLS

In today's competitive job market, you will want to recognize and take advantage of all your skills. Knowing your transferable skills can translate into a promotion or help facilitate a transfer into an entirely new job, especially one that involves a new industry or new occupation. Knowing which of your skills are transferable and emphasizing them will help you convince managers you are capable of making a positive transition.

What exactly are transferable skills? Here are some examples:

- Leadership and self-discipline
- Teamwork and motivation
- Problem solving and negotiation skills
- Adaptability and flexibility
- Scope of knowledge
- Organizational or project management
- Passion, enthusiasm and commitment to excellence

Transferable skills are usually not listed on job descriptions or job postings, yet they can make a big difference in employment selection and promotions.

THE MARKETING OF YOU – WHAT IS YOUR PERSONAL BRAND?

Before Tom Peters, author of the book, *In Search of Excellence*, crafted the term "personal brand", it was known simply as "professional reputation". Once you've established your career direction, you must begin to think much like a sales and marketing professional, which starts with branding yourself. Personal branding is mandatory in the New World of Work!

✞✞✞

"It's a new brand world. You're branded, branded, branded. We are CEO's of our own companies: Me Inc. To be in business today, our most important job is to be head marketer for the brand called You."

TOM PETERS – WRITER ON BUSINESS MANAGEMENT ISSUES

✞✞✞

Who makes your favorite car, clothes, or cell phone? What beverage comes to mind when you need a pick-me-up? Each of these questions involves your reaction to a particular brand. A 'brand' is a collection of assumptions about quality, appeal, and reliability that you've made in response to repeated experience with a variety of people, products, or services. As an example, you easily recognize the Campbell Soup logo in grocery stores. Regardless of your opinion of Campbell or their soup, the company has large brand recognition. In fact, many people would be surprised to know that in 2013 Campbell sold over 200 million cans of chicken noodle soup in the U.S. alone.[42] Obviously, their customers feel strongly about the quality and function of the product, and Campbell Soup invested heavily in their branding efforts to achieve this success.

> ### Ca•reer•ology
> *Any step toward a new career goal is a good step, even if it is a small one. It's important to get out of your comfort zone. Put a stake in the ground and start walking toward it. It's a great relief and also motivational just to be moving!*

In the New World of Work, we need to prudently market ourselves as if we were a company or product to achieve career success. Whether you know it or not, if you've been in the working world for any length of time, you already have a personal brand. Go on the Internet and Google yourself. You are already there in cyberspace. In many cases, a recruiter looking to fill a position will Google your name, even before looking at your resume.

Your brand must tell people the benefit they will receive when they purchase or acquire what you have to offer. Ultimately, you are the one who is bringing this resource to the marketplace. The key is to turn your strengths, skills and accomplishments into an image that is compelling to your network and employers. The Internet makes it easy for you to define and manage your personal brand. Also with the Internet, you can easily observe how others are successfully branding themselves.

CREATING AN EFFECTIVE PERSONAL BRAND

Unlike a major company, the good news is that you do not have to spend a lot of money on your personal branding efforts. Most of the work involves capturing important attributes about your work history and career assets that will appeal to future employers (and perhaps your current employer for promotion). The basic platforms for this are your resume or curriculum vitae (CV), your business card, and a LinkedIn online profile. LinkedIn and other online programs can help you brand yourself by adding resume content and listing information relevant to your brand.

Begin your branding development process by asking yourself key questions, such as:

- What are my best skills and accomplishments?
- How am I currently perceived by others, inside and outside of my immediate network?
- What career direction do I want to go in?
- How do I want to be perceived in the future?

> ## Ca•reer•ology
>
> *What does your current brand convey? Does it convey a message, an ideology, a service, a style, a quality of life?*

Some additional questions include:

- Are your written materials (Resume/CV, LinkedIn, etc.) current, relevant, and interesting to read?
- Are you posting interesting questions and providing insight to your network?
- Do you have a compelling Personal Value Statement (PVS) or Elevator Pitch?
- Have you asked a mentor, friend or career coach to help you to improve your written and oral presentation?
- Have you read some materials on personal branding or books on marketing?

Answer each question with a critical eye. Seek opinions from trusted friends/family and/or a professional career coach/writer. Next, create a brief story about yourself and your career interests. See yourself as being the person you want to be. Make "I" statements and write in the present tense. For example: Financial Analyst: "*I am an expert analyst in the consumer foods industry. I produce quality reports on time, and I work well with teams in rapidly changing environments.*"

Think about your abilities and skills. If you are able to convey noteworthy attributes in your oral statements and written materials, who wouldn't want to interview you and perhaps hire you? Most of your competitors will not have spent the time to build their personal brand and you will have a leg up for career opportunities if you do.

The book, *Career Distinction: Stand Out by Building Your Brand*, by William Arruda and Kirsten Dixson, is an excellent resource on this subject.[43] The step-by-step guide covers the stories of several individuals who have succeeded with personal branding efforts.

WRITING A GREAT RESUME AND LINKEDIN PROFILE

Despite the many years resumes have been around, there are still ongoing debates about proper design. Fortunately, there is less confusion about how an online profile should be written. With LinkedIn profiles, much of the format is pre-established, and you don't have to spend time worrying about formatting details. Make sure your resume and online profiles are professional and inspiring, not boring. Not a great writer? Updating your materials can be overwhelming. If this is the case, hire a professional who can help. Good writing can make all the difference in the world.

Over 95% of recruiters use LinkedIn for finding job candidates. Your resume and online profile will be the broadest and best representation of who you are. These are the foundations of your personal branding tools.

Important Messaging for Your Resume and LinkedIn Profile
1. Who You Are (Lead with character)
2. How You Think (Problem solving, etc.)
3. What You Have Done (Accomplishments)

"An online media profile is just as much, if not more important than a resume."
DANA AND PAUL

✞✞✞

MORE RESUME AND LINKEDIN FUNDAMENTALS

1. **Know Your Audience**. Your resume should be narrow-casted to specific individuals or groups. The content and length will depend upon whether you are sending it to your network for referrals or applying for a specific position, in which case you should do some tailoring. On the other hand, your LinkedIn profile is essentially a broadcast, available for review by several hundred million people across the globe. Your LinkedIn content and length will generally remain the same, except for periodic updates.

2. **Be Creative and Customize**. This is your branding. Your resume must be adaptable and interesting. Make sure to customize your resume for each position you apply for, using the prospective company's jargon. To make it easier to customize, create a separate document that lists all of your major achievements. Outline your achievements in a Situation/Task/Action/Result (or S.T.A.R.) format. S.T.A.R.'s are brief statements outlining a work scenario (situation or task) you found yourself in or initiated, the steps (actions) you took to solve the problem or capitalize on the opportunity, and the outcomes (results) of your activity.

3. **Be Consistent**. Be sure your resume and LinkedIn profile contents are in alignment with each other to convey the same message about your personal brand. Recruiters will look at both, and you don't want to create uncertainty or confusion about who you are and what you do. Are you a programmer or a systems analyst? If you've held both jobs and your resume seems to emphasize one over the other from your LinkedIn profile, the recruiter or hiring manager may become confused and move on to someone else. Also, be sure your LinkedIn headliner aligns with your LinkedIn Summary to avoid confusion. It's understandable that you will have some differences between the two, but 80% of your messaging should be the same from one medium to the other.

Sample S.T.A.R. Questions For Developing Your Own Customized Resume Content

S (Situation) – What was the situation?

- Managed a new software release called "OS-8".
- Recognized a lack of volunteers in church's food ministry.

T (Task) – What did I do?

- Wrote code using HTML, supervising two programmers.
- Proposed a detailed plan to church leaders to attract additional volunteers.

A (Action) – How did I do it?

- Developed code and successfully tested in a six month timeframe.
- Designed a recruitment campaign for the ministry.

R (Result) – What happened?

- Released software on time, within budget, and made $5 million in revenue.
- Recruited successfully five new volunteers in six months to the ministry.

Download this template at www.careeringbook.com.

---

4. **Have a Scanable Resume**. In addition to having a paper resume, you need an electronic one that is easily scanable. This is very important because most recruiters will use the latest imaging technology, allowing them to store resumes in databases and then search through many applicants electronically. Recruiters are frequently searching LinkedIn for candidates and doing so primarily through keyword search software. Be sure your content includes the industry and job buzzwords to get their attention. These technologies usually take the form of Optical Character Recognition (OCR) or Internet Bots, which are automated programs customized to systematically browse the web and extract information based upon keywords. **Tip:** Put extra keywords in white font in the margin areas of your resume. The bots will pick these up, which will increase your chances of success. Knowing how the

keyword searches work and taking action can help keep you in the game.

Key Elements to an Effective Resume

1. Lead with an inspiring Profile or Summary.
2. Include achievements that tell your story (Situation–Task–Action–Results or S.T.A.R.) – Competencies.
3. Focus on key responsibilities – not just descriptions of each job.
4. Tell the truth – but make the truth interesting.
5. Create a powerful, visually appealing resume in Microsoft Word and PDF.
6. Be succinct, but use appropriate keywords throughout the document.
7. Have additional formatted material ready for the 'cut and paste' sections of online applications.
8. Prepare multiple resumes refined to your various target audiences.

> **Ca•reer•ology**
>
> *Mentors and mentoring can be worth as much as a college education and perhaps a decade or more of income. Be sure to find trusted, accomplished mentors to help guide you with your decision-making, outlook, networking, and behaviors. And, do the same for someone else!*

Avoid Common Pitfalls of a LinkedIn Profile

1. Images, photos, videos and other images must be professional.
2. Headline – make it interesting, but not gimmicky. It should convey who you are and what you do.
3. Have a clear URL. Sample: www.linkedin.com/in/johnsmith/.
4. Complete your profile as much as you can. Fill in all sections. Use keywords throughout.
5. Your Summary should tell the viewer what you offer by way of expertise, and example. Using first person pronouns, such as I, my, we, our, are acceptable.
6. Describe each position held in concise but thorough fashion.
7. Include achievements that tell your story (Situation–Task–Action–Results or S.T.A.R.) – Competencies.

8. Keep your profile updated and fresh.
9. Have at least 50 reputable first (1st) connections.
10. Give and earn endorsements and recommendations.

THE POWER OF A STRONG NETWORK

In business, networking allows you to ultimately get what you want or need by helping others get what they want or need. How important is networking? From a career standpoint, this is like asking, "Do I really need to eat this week?" or, "If I run out of gas in my car, will it keep running?"

Networking is critical! Everything you've heard about the importance of networking is true. It is the essence of career success in the New World of Work. In fact, studies show that upwards of 80% of all private sector jobs are found through networking.[44] That's the majority of the way most positions are filled—despite the perception that most jobs are filled via online job posts. A job often starts as a need in the mind of a person within an organization. This could be anyone, but you will likely hear titles like hiring manager or human resources professional.

"Networking is more about 'farming' than about 'hunting'.
It's about cultivating relationships."
DR. IVAN MISNER – FOUNDER AND CHAIRMAN BUSINESS NETWORK INTERNATIONAL

Through careful networking, you may learn of a job opening before it's publicized. How do you find this 'crystal ball' that may help you uncover job opportunities before they are even posted? It's through advance proactive networking, conducted on a regular basis. Unfortunately, thousands of people who became downsized or laid off during the Great Recession had little to no professional network when they were terminated. In many cases, the few people within their network also got laid off. This left them with no network, outside of family and friends.

YOU NEED TO DIG YOUR WELL - IN ADVANCE!

Harvey Mackay is a business leader, speaker and author who wrote a NY Times bestselling book about networking called *Dig Your Well Before You're Thirsty – The Only Networking Book You'll Ever Need.*[45]

Mackay gives examples of building and organizing a network of relationships to enhance both your career and life. His book is helpful to those who are new to the business world and also for experienced professionals who want a refresher.

Networking can and should occur anywhere: at church, in associations, informal groups, with neighbors, on and offline. Mackay points out that one of the best places to network and develop key networking skills is at a local Toastmasters Club. A Toastmasters meeting is not just about making speeches. It's about doing your homework, self-confidence, appearance and becoming an interesting person. Actually, any job loss or layoff is a networking opportunity. People don't normally want to know about your pain, but some will be inspired by how you are handling your challenge of finding work. This is an opportunity to enlist them in what could become your next exciting career exploration journey. Do not let seemingly negative circumstances control your outlook for a renewed mission in your life and work!

How to Network? It's Not All About You

By becoming known as a person who is authentic about helping others, you will be successful at networking. When meeting new people, be sincere and let them know you want to help. Get to know their needs before asking them for help with yours. Always offer to return any favors your contacts provide and be sure to communicate with them even at times when you don't need their support. Your reputation will grow as a contributor and don't be surprised when others reciprocate with contacts, ideas and encouragement.

"I've learned that people will forget what you said, people will forget what you did, but people will never forget how you made them feel."
Maya Angelou – American Author And Poet

Your faith must be strong, and you must maintain your spirit regardless of whether you receive anything in return. It's not about you. Help may not come right away and will likely not come from someone you have helped directly, but rather from another person—someone unexpected. You never know! When networking, simply saying hello, stating your name and smiling makes you approachable.

NETWORKING: LISTEN MORE – TALK LESS

Becoming an active listener is a vital skill to master. How well you listen has a major impact on your job effectiveness, and on the quality of your relationships with others. The way to improve your listening skills is to practice active listening. This is where you not only make a conscious effort to hear the words that another person is saying, but more importantly, try to understand the underlying messages being sent.

✤✤✤

"You can make more friends in two months by becoming really interested in other people than you can in two years by trying to get other people interested in you."[46]
DALE CARNEGIE – BESTSELLING AUTHOR

✤✤✤

Listen with both head and heart, and you will be amazed at the powerful response, especially if you paraphrase the other person's statement. Consider, for example: "John, it sounds like you're burned out on the legal field and that you are seriously considering a career change?" Notice that the listener demonstrated how well they listened in repeating back the response. When people talk to a good listener, it makes them feel respected. Sometimes people will ask you directly for your help and advice. This is a compliment and a great opportunity to build a relationship. Do whatever you can to follow through and help them make a key connection. Sincerity develops trust and creates a bond that can lead to new contacts, friends and even champions for you. Try it. You do not have to be outgoing to do this. You just need to have an open, responsive and giving heart.

NETWORKING WITH RECRUITERS

Connecting with recruiters sounds like a logical thing to do, especially if you are in job search. After all, a recruiter's job is to place qualified candidates with client companies, right? They might have an open position that you would be a great match for. Correct? This may or may not be true, so your initial contact with them might be just pure networking. You might get fortunate, but they most likely will not have immediate opportunities for you. They may help you connect with other networkers, but opportunities will probably come later, especially if you find a way to help them. Ask what other key jobs they are seeking to fill and offer to help connect them with your contacts. This is a foundation for building a solid relationship with recruiters.

NETWORKING AND YOUR PERSONAL VALUE STATEMENT (PVS)

When networking as a job seeker, be sure to tell your story, briefly and passionately. We call this your Personal Value Statement or Elevator Pitch. As an example, when meeting a new contact and being asked what you do:"I am a product manager with 15 years accomplishments in consumer foods. Do you know anyone who could use my talents to drive sales? I can help companies, such as HJ Heinz, Nabisco, or Coca-Cola improve their revenues of key products."

Another good tactic in networking is to seek out master networkers. These are people who have a large network of contacts. Typically, they are in sales, client-facing jobs, such as insurance agents, real estate brokers, and bankers. Be genuine when you connect with people and be candid in sharing your situation, letting them know that you respect their position and appreciate their time. Don't try to be someone you are not. Remember to diversify—associate with more than one demographic or group.

> **Ca•reer•ology**
>
> *Connecting with master networkers can significantly improve your efficiency in networking.*

A book that offers state-of-the-art career management guidance is *The Start–Up of You*[47], by Reid Hoffman and Ben Casnocha. Reid Hoffman is one of the founders of LinkedIn. In addition to the importance of "network building", they also clarify the fact that all careers are undergoing constant change. The authors support the belief that lifetime employment and training by one employer is gone. Therefore, you must take ownership of your career by preparing for the future through continuous networking.

ONLINE SOCIAL MEDIA NETWORKING

Networking while working in your current job must be a critical part of your career management plan and can be started by using social media. Numerous online resources are available to make new contacts and understand changes occurring in the business world. They include LinkedIn, Google+, Meetup groups, video conferencing, and blogging to less formal online tools, such as Facebook, Instagram, and Twitter.

Within the New World of Work, it is important to be proactive by asking yourself the following: "How is my job and industry going to change over the coming years? What do I need to learn this year? Who do I need to know to be prepared to make a job change within my company or elsewhere?" These questions should be considered regardless of whether you are an assistant, manager, engineer, accountant, or executive. Be sure to follow online Influencers. These are key industry leaders whose material can help you remain informed, coached, and perhaps inspired about trends in every industry. These are professionals who are heavily followed and who are considered thought leaders on LinkedIn and in periodicals and articles. Monitoring Influencers is essential to your personal development efforts and your career success.

"There is no substitute for personal contact."
DWIGHT D. EISENHOWER – 34TH PRESIDENT OF THE UNITED STATES

✢✢✢

YOUR PROFESSIONAL NETWORK QUALITY AND QUANTITY

It is important to remember to deepen as many of your relationships through live interaction as possible. This includes coffees and lunches for local contacts and online video for those removed geographically. Any form of interactive contact is beneficial. Capitalizing on all these resources can seem like an overwhelming process. Start with a few functions each month and build from there.

What are the characteristics of an ideal network contact? Generally, they exhibit the following:

- ✓ They reciprocate.
- ✓ They give freely without expectations.
- ✓ They exhibit high character.
- ✓ They offer demonstrated expertise.
- ✓ They are professional.
- ✓ They are well-connected themselves.

✓ They are diverse from one another.

Can friends be part of your professional network? Sure! They should ideally have a profession and some expertise, along with the other characteristics above, but do not exclude friends from being part of your professional network. Below are some helpful tips from Anthony V. Edwards, Sr. Software Architect Manager, on the dynamics of effective networking:

Top Ten Reasons Why I Network
1. I find people interesting.
2. I find people worthwhile.
3. I hope to help them someday.
4. I hope they can help me someday.
5. I enjoy hearing others' stories.
6. I appreciate learning from others' successes/failures.
7. I like sharing my successes/failures with others.
8. I enjoy reminiscing past times together.
9. I enjoy connecting people I know.
10. I enjoy sharing time with a friend over a hot drink.

How I Network
* Catch a coffee (no agenda conversation).
* Phone a friend (a call with a purpose).
* Drop a line (a quick question, a forwarded news item, a personal update).

When I Network
* I listen attentively and take notes.
* Contribute relevantly and make suggestions.
* Follow-up on promised actions.
* Relax and enjoy each other's company.

Networking Quality
* At an event, I try to limit each conversation to 10 minutes. If I want to take longer, that sounds like an opportunity to plan a coffee together.
* When working 40 hours, I try to network twice a week. When between client engagements, I limit myself to two coffees a day at most.
* I try to stay in touch every few months if feasible.

- I separate professional networking (e.g. LinkedIn) from personal networking. (e.g. charitable work).
- Be true to my professional self.

Reflection

There are a number of opinions about how many people should be in your network. The answer is dependent upon your desires, ability to manage contacts, and interests. For some, as few as 50 high quality contacts may suffice. For others, a few thousand may be more appropriate. If you want a wide reach, having a large number in your network will not hurt. Try to add a minimum of two or three new people per month.

> ## Ca•reer•ology
>
> *Regardless of how you choose to build your professional network, it's important to be selective. Be sure the other person is an appropriate contact for you.*

1. What organizations can you connect with to immediately start expanding your network?
2. Who would make an ideal person? Would their background and mindset be a helpful addition for your network?
3. Don't forget your spouse's network. Who in your spouse's network would make an ideal addition to your network?

YOUR JOB LEADS ARE NOT FAR AWAY

Most people have heard about the idea of six degrees of separation. This theory promotes the idea that everyone on the planet, in terms of a personal connection, is only six relationships or fewer away from one another. Hence, your network of contacts can serve as an easy way to reach several people who can help with job search, contracts, or at least leads and referrals. The key is to continue to cultivate and manage your network through regular contact. Ask your network contacts for an update on their situations and close with yours. This allows you to remind them of your work or business and could lead to opportunities for everyone. This actively promotes your ongoing branding efforts discussed earlier.

LinkedIn is currently the easiest and most effective online resource for finding new connections, tracking existing ones and communicating directly.

It provides a great way for you to find key hiring decision-makers and offers a vehicle to contact them.

The following chart illustrates the results of a relationship study. This study determined that most people found their new job opportunity from contacts they saw occasionally and rarely in over 82% of the time. In other words, the contacts were considered weak ties or distant relationships.[48]

Relationship Study: The Strength of Weak Ties

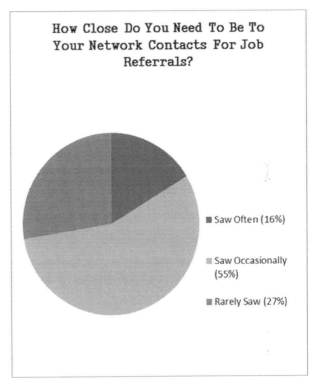

How Close Do You Need To Be To Your Network Contacts For Job Referrals?

- Saw Often (16%)
- Saw Occasionally (55%)
- Rarely Saw (27%)

STAY RELEVANT – COMPETENCIES

To remain competitive, you must continuously retrain, renew, and reinvent yourself. Seek out training and development opportunities. Don't be afraid to invest your own money into important educational efforts. Many universities and community colleges offer a variety of programs designed to help you remain attractive from an employment or consultant standpoint. Some of these programs are free to unemployed and under-employed adult students. Additionally, there are lots of online resources, free information, including white papers, TED Talks, videos and downloadable programs that are instantly available.

A big problem today is that many are not ready to move forward and act when the opportunity presents itself. In fact, according to a national survey, eighty-three percent (83%) of employees had been passed over for promotion because management felt they couldn't make the necessary changes to move to the next level of their career.[49] Participate in programs that will stretch your knowledge or skill base and that will give you an advantage over the competition. The goal is to become well-rounded and to grow in your personal brand.

"Develop a passion for learning. If you do, you will never cease to grow."
ANTHONY J.D'ANGELO - AUTHOR

Below is list of action steps that can help you become more effective in your managing your career. Copy the steps into your smartphone and copy/paste them on your wall or refrigerator. Review them periodically and practice them until they become habits.

10 Ways to Become a More Effective Professional

1. Continuously improve your communications skills.
2. Be technologically savvy.
3. Obtain broader and deeper knowledge.
4. Consistently perform quality work.
5. Show genuine interest. Be engaged in the entire process.
6. Take responsibility for your actions.
7. Have an innovative, free agent mindset.
8. Be adaptable to unanticipated changes.
9. Be authentic. Treat others with respect and dignity.
10. Brainstorm and provide alternative solutions to problems.

CAREER PLANNING FOR OLDER WORKERS

Looking for work when you are over 55 can be especially challenging. A 30-something millennial hiring manager may look at you with hesitation. In his or her eyes, you may appear to be out of touch with technology and current business practices. You must do everything you can to avoid this perception or bias.

You may offer a wealth of knowledge and have a great work ethic that can substantially help an employer. The key is to be professional and current in every regard—from your technology skills to your LinkedIn profile to your selection of dress and eyewear. If you don't have a LinkedIn profile, then make it a priority to create one while you are updating your resume. In the New World of Work, you need both. We cannot stress enough the importance of creating a well-developed and expressive LinkedIn profile. Perception is reality, and with extra effort you can create a positive impression. Your intellectual value, principles, and work ethic offer a wealth of resources that, if properly channeled into a new employment environment, can become a winning combination for you and the employer.

The Council for Adult and Experiential Learning Foundation (CAEL) – in concert with the U.S. Department of Labor, conducted a program called Tapping Mature Talent in 2009 – 2012.[50] Despite the employment crisis during the Great Recession, they found that older workers, who followed a professional or best practices approach to job search, had a respectable job placement rate. The best practices included:

- Obtaining certification(s)
- Branding themselves
- Having a mentor, career coach, etc.
- Computer and technology training
- Accepting unpaid adult internships – Don't be afraid to volunteer initially.

In selling yourself to hiring managers, be sure to illustrate your past accomplishments and current skills that demonstrate immediate and future value to the company or department's mission. There are many online training and education programs available today to bolster your background. Certifications will give your efforts even more credibility with hiring managers and recruiters. Some of these are provided at a minimal cost, sometimes at no cost, for those who are unemployed or under-employed. Check with your favorite associations, state agencies, and conduct online searches for certificate or certification programs. Available at community colleges and even universities,

Ca•reer•ology

With thousands of Baby Boomers exiting the workplace every day, some employers are worried about a 'brain drain', which may very well spell opportunities for older workers who want to continue to work.

certificate programs are becoming a way for workers young and old, to jump-start careers.

An alternative to seeking traditional employment is to become a consultant and/or a full-fledged entrepreneur. These avenues can be rewarding, but they require you to have deep-seated characteristics such as:

- High energy
- Risk-taker
- Visionary leader
- Detail-oriented when appropriate
- Quick learner
- Emotional strength
- Marketing mentality

A helpful resource for comprehensive planning of your next steps in life and career is *The New Retirementality,* by Mitch Anthony.[51] The book encourages readers to challenge the traditional assumption about retiring at the ages of 62 or 65 and no longer working. Instead, Anthony challenges us to think about creating a life that is both fulfilling and flexible, based upon individual desires. He suggests we stay in the game—be active from paid or unpaid opportunities—regardless of age. A resource for considering entrepreneurship is *Escape from Corporate America: A Practical Guide to Creating the Career of Your Dreams,* by Pamela Skillings.[52]

As an experienced worker, you are in a unique position to help others. After all, the foundational principles behind success on a personal and work level all lie on values and principles that continue to provide results today: organization, discipline, commitment, flexibility, honesty, responsibility, accountability and much more. Consider becoming a mentor—any kind; it does not matter. Your service could be offered to younger people, the elderly, or someone near your own age. Perhaps you can help with Careering issues described in this book or something else unrelated to your career. You get to choose based upon your interests and talents. The needs in our country are extensive. Mentoring can provide enormous benefits to recipients and will not only provide you with an immeasurable feeling of fulfillment, but place you in an environment where you will be privy to information, networking opportunities, and in proximity to influential contacts.

CAREER PLANNING FOR A YOUNGER WORKER

If you cannot find your ideal job right away, get going with some kind of work, even if it's unskilled. To supplement his work as a professional body builder, Arnold Schwarzenegger was a bricklayer before he became a highly paid actor and later Governor of California. You will feel better earning a paycheck, and it is easier finding a new job while you are already in the workforce.

Another path to meaningful employment is through unpaid internships or volunteering. This could be a vital step in gaining the experience and contacts needed to make a career change or get back into the workforce after a break. Adding new responsibilities to your resume from an internship can make you a more attractive job candidate.

> **Ca•reer•ology**
>
> *Be very careful with your personal social media network activities and keep them separate from your professional network activities.*

This is how Jim and Norma, our two case studies from earlier chapters in this book, and members of our St. Andrews Career Network Ministry, found meaningful employment. If you can convince an employer to offer you such an option, this is a great way for the company to get to know your capabilities and also permit you to obtain some valuable experience and contacts. Donating your time, in many cases, will bring forth an income opportunity to you sooner rather than later.

Prior to beginning your job search, be sure to have your marketing materials complete. This includes your resume and online profiles, such as LinkedIn. If you don't have a LinkedIn profile, then make it a priority to create one while you are developing your resume. In this New World of Work, you need a resume and a LinkedIn profile.

If you do not have a lot of relevant work experience, your activities at school, part-time jobs, hobbies, and especially volunteer activities, are all appropriate for your resume and online profiles. If you are not a great writer, consider investing in a professional writer, at least for editing. The cost will pay for itself. Be sure to build your network of professional contacts and don't be afraid to ask them for advice. Asking for advice rather than for a specific job is a very effective way to engage someone. People love to give advice. If you ask them or imply that you are desperately in need of a job, this, in most cases, will put them on the defensive and is not a sound foundation for building a professional relationship.

A classic book for identifying your career interests and creating an effective job search is the all-time bestseller *What Color Is Your Parachute?*, by Richard N. Bolles.[53] Bolles provides a detailed way to analyze career options in light of your natural talents and personal interests. He also addresses the spiritual part of career management.

Finally, allocate time to find a couple of mentors. This could involve finding a volunteer mentor or even hiring one to serve as a career coach. An experienced mentor can help walk you through your career and job exploration. While you may think this is unnecessary, the end result could make all the difference you'll need to be successful.

VOLUNTEERING CHANGES LIVES – INCLUDING YOUR OWN!

For some, the idea of volunteering personal talents and time can seem a bit overwhelming. Many people today lead extremely busy lives, and if you have not volunteered before, fitting such a task into a hectic schedule might appear to be unrealistic. Yes, it can be difficult to do when you are working, but still possible. If you are out of work, you have no excuse not to be volunteering.

"Don't get tired of helping others. You will be rewarded when the time is right, if you don't give up."
GALATIANS, 6:9

Almost anyone who has done volunteer work will tell you how volunteering can fit into your schedule and that the rewards from volunteering are immeasurable. You receive the satisfaction of helping someone, and also volunteering is a great way to network. Where should you volunteer? Begin by investigating needs in your community based on your interests. Once you find an organization that aligns with your personal values, contact them. By becoming involved, you will have the opportunity to demonstrate your skills and make new contacts for your network and expand your personal brand.

Dear Heavenly Father,

I lift up my career and ask You for guidance. Help me to step out on faith to pursue dreams and use the skills You have blessed me with so that others will know You are for and with me.

I pray for progression in my life and that of my family. Direct my footsteps according to Your perfect will and enable me to pursue the appropriate career path.

Grant me favor in the eyes of my superiors and bless the work of my hands. Father, let Your Spirit of wisdom, understanding, counsel, power, knowledge and fear of the Lord rest upon me.

In Jesus' Name I pray.

Amen

Sample Scenario:
Mary is an under-employed CPA working for a coal mining company and struggling with her career. Below is her plan of action.

Chapter 3 Key Activities Worksheet
Who Am I and How Am I Perceived?

A. Research companies in other industries.

What? *Search for jobs in accounting using Google and LinkedIn.*

By When? *Next week*

B. Network building and intelligence gathering.

What? *Attend 1 or 3 social or business meetings*

By When? *Every week, beginning next week*

C. Build skills, training and branding.

What? *Hire a life/career coach to help with direction*

By When? *Obtain referrals next two weeks & get going!*

D. Build in volunteering, family and fun.

What? *Help at a local food pantry; take family on an outing to local state park*

By When? *Volunteer this week / family outing, next week.*

Your Turn: *Completing this form will provide you with valuable insights and action steps.*

Chapter 3 Key Activities Worksheet
Who Am I and How Am I Perceived?

A. Research companies in other industries.

What? _____
_____
_____
_____

By When? _____

B. Network building and intelligence gathering.

What? _____
_____
_____
_____

By When? _____

C. Build skills, training and branding.

What? _____
_____
_____
_____

By When? _____

D. Build in volunteering, family and fun.

What? _____
_____
_____
_____

By When? _____

Download additional templates at www.careeringbook.com

Notes & Thoughts

Notes & Thoughts

Seek and You Shall Find!

CHAPTER 4: JOB SEARCH STRATEGIES

Seek and You Shall Find!

–INTRODUCTION–

Searching for work can be filled with anticipation, anxiety, and stress. Are you presently concerned about or have you been frustrated with a job search? If so, you are not alone. Let's say you've applied for dozens of jobs that are perfect for you, and you receive no feedback—nothing! You call friends who have jobs or contracts at good companies, and despite their best efforts, they are unable to give you any good news—nothing! You dress up, print some resumes, and go to a job fair where you meet several representatives from great companies—and again you hear nothing! Don't give up! Your success will depend on your willingness to do the things unsuccessful people are often not willing to do—in this case being outgoing and persistent. Upon reading this chapter, you will know how to develop a job search campaign, be better equipped and inspired, which will lead you on a very rewarding and meaningful path.

THIS IS NOT THE TIME TO BE MEEK, FOR THE MEEK WILL 'PROBABLY NOT' GET THE INTERVIEW!

✠✠✠

"Knock and the door will be opened to you"
MATTHEW 7:7–8

✠✠✠

DEVELOP A GREAT SEARCH CAMPAIGN

Developing a formal search campaign will help propel you. Once you have your campaign outlined in writing, you will feel better about your situation and what you need to be successful. Keep your plan in front of you to help you stay focused. Your earlier research work from Chapter 3: Your Career Plan and Personal Brand will help you build the foundation of your campaign. You will have determined what type of work you should be pursuing and what the outlook, pay and benefits look like for that work. There will be some disappointments as you begin to execute your plan, but be sure to give yourself credit for milestones—contacts made and Thank You notes sent. Include these in your list of gratitudes. We know that a good campaign will provide you with interviews that can lead to opportunities. You may even encounter a remarkable new job opportunity that you could never have imagined.

> ## Ca•reer•ology
> *The 'Hidden Job Market' refers to the 'unadvertised' job market. One major element of this is the simple time lag that occurs in the processing of a job post from internal preparation and approvals until it is made public. This gives known, "unofficial candidates," an advantage.*

WHAT DOES A POWERFUL JOB OR CONTRACT CAMPAIGN LOOK LIKE?

Whether you are seeking a traditional job or other form of work, the elements of your search campaign will be the same. To be successful, you must treat this effort as a full-time job. Start your day as if you are reporting to work. You must fully commit to doing this. Your home office is now your campaign headquarters. We know it's hard, especially from home. To help you feel like you're at work, dress nicely. Let your family know you are working, and you are not to be disturbed, except during some break times throughout the day.

The first step in the search process begins with gathering facts about opportunities and relationships. You can do this using the Internet, phone, email, and in conversation with friends, neighbors and through face-to-face meetings. Notice that we did not say, "Get on the Internet and apply to every applicable job posting with your cover letter and resume." This 'Hit Submit' mentality can be a big problem. Although a necessary portion of your job search, applying for jobs online has been shown to produce few results and can waste your valuable time. Many jobs that are posted are done so only as a formality after the position has been open internally for a period of time, or after an internal leading candidate—or someone else with an inside track—has been identified. Indeed, statistics show the majority of jobs and contracts are found through networking.

✚✚✚

"Your thoughts drive your emotions. Your emotions drive your actions.
Your actions drive your results."
WELDON LONG – NY TIMES BESTSELLING AUTHOR, SPEAKER

✚✚✚

Before you begin your job search, do your homework. You must know what you want! The process of discovering what you want is outlined in Chapter 3: Your Career Plan and Personal Brand and further explored in Chapter 7: Life and Career Purpose. The danger of not understanding what you want is that you could undergo an unfocused search, leading to unhappiness, wasted energy, and frustration.

DANA'S JOB LOSS, MAJOR ILLNESS AND HIS WILLPOWER

In his own words: Below is a true story from co-author Dana Gower about how his desire to find new work during a disability resulted in success.

When It Rains, It Pours, and Dana Had No Umbrella!

The first half of 2009 was a very difficult time for my family and me. Not only had I had lost my job with a start-up firm a few months earlier, my now ex-wife had relocated out of state with our two young teenagers. I was devastated by the loss of day-to-day contact with my kids and worried about re-establishing work amid a growing recession.

Things Go from Bad to Worse

In February, I became bedridden from a rare autoimmune disease that resulted in chronic fatigue, pain and extreme weight loss of 50 lbs. over 2 1/2 months. Among other issues, I landed in the hospital for several days. After my release, I could not prospect for work very easily and could hardly walk. The few times I did go out in public, I looked like a concentration camp victim—hardly employable! Fortunately, my girlfriend, extended family, and dedicated friends gave me everything I needed to begin to recover physically and some financial support as well. Despite this aid, I began to get behind on bills. I was neither old enough nor otherwise eligible to withdraw from my pension. I felt worthless but determined to recover.

Good News – Dana Gets a Phone Call

A surprising turn of events: I got a call from a former colleague at the start-up firm I had worked for previously. He said the owner had created a national investment management practice that he was no longer interested in running. It even included a planned roll-out of what would be my own mutual fund! Would I like to take over the business on favorable terms? I couldn't believe it. I warned them about how I looked but that my doctors said I would recover, albeit slowly. They asked me if I could start within a few weeks. Meanwhile, two of my brothers had just arranged to have me flown to Maine, where my dear mom would look after me. She found food that had some appeal to my impaired taste buds. My sister took me to her integrative health doctor. My dad provided moral and financial support from Nevada. I tried to push back the start date but an important board meeting was scheduled in Arizona, and I needed to be there. So I returned to Raleigh where the owner took me to buy a new business suit to fit my frail body, and I got on a plane to Arizona with him. I felt dizzy most of the time as I crept along at a snail's pace. Fortunately, he did most of the talking at the meeting, and the deal was done.

A New Start and Lessons Learned

At the stroke of a pen and with little more than basic willpower to show up at my new office each morning, my life began to turn around. I was able to catch up on many of my past due bills and restart a savings account. This provided the means for regular visits with all my kids, including my young teenagers. Likewise, my health and fitness ultimately turned around. This took away a lot of the 'bad' feelings and allowed me to feel pretty darn good! However, as if previously losing my family was not difficult enough, the job loss served as a reminder of the pain, disappointment, anger, defeat and injury I had already experienced. On a personal level, comparing one pain to the other, I would much rather go through job and career setbacks than the human loss of my identity as husband and father.

Reflection

Dana learned that sometimes opportunities unfold in unexpected ways. One slight shift in circumstance and perspective can make all the difference. He believed his desire and effort to try to return to work, even while very sick, combined with help and grace from God, provided these unexpected opportunities for him.

1. During his illness, what elements of Dana's mindset can you identify that made a difference in how he overcame his physical obstacles?
2. What can you learn about the personal and professional network of family, friends, and business acquaintances that Dana had around him? How important were these people to his spirit and well-being?
3. How did Dana turn a challenge into an opportunity that resulted in restoring physical contact with his children?

DEVISE YOUR SEARCH CAMPAIGN – BE BOLD!

Unless you've worked in marketing or politics, you probably never thought about your job search as a campaign. They are very similar. In fact, a professional search process can be taken straight from the playbook used in both professions. What does a successful job/contract search campaign look like?

"Energy and persistence conquer all things."
BENJAMIN FRANKLIN – U.S. FOUNDING FATHER, AUTHOR, STATESMAN

In the job search mission, as long as your skills and experience are current, steadily following the proven formula above will lead you to success. You may even be fortunate enough to land an opportunity soon after your launch begins. More likely, it will take more time than you would prefer. Some of the action steps may feel foreign to you, especially if you've never served in a sales or marketing role, and even harder if you are introverted. However, reminding yourself about the potential payoff from performing these activities will energize you.

While you are executing your campaign, remember you will be communicating with both new and existing network contacts. Use your time and their time wisely. Diligently following up or staying in touch does not mean you are making a pest of yourself. If you have trouble connecting by phone, email, or text, then write a note. If still no response, then it's time to ask yourself if those people are truly dedicated networkers. Good things will happen as you get in the groove of executing your campaign. The chart on the next page, 'A Proven Success Formula for Your Search Campaign' lists five critical steps that we know will help you land the right opportunity. Take daily actions toward accomplishing your objectives. This can be difficult, and you may feel like it is a waste of time. You can be assured that it is not! Each time you complete another action, you will feel better knowing that you are getting things done, moving you closer to your goal. Change oftentimes happens in small increments. Stick with it!

Reflection

Implementing a comprehensive job search can be very difficult, especially if you do not enjoy promoting yourself. Most people will go through ups and downs, and the thought of this effort can be daunting, especially if you tend to be shy. Extroverts generally have it easier!

A good book to help you with overcoming introversion is *Self-Promotion for Introverts: The Quiet Guide to Getting Ahead*, written by Nancy Ancowitz.[54]

1. How can you rise above a quiet, introverted nature to undertake a promotional effort?
2. Where can you go to help yourself open up and become more proactive in doing what does not come naturally to you?

A Proven Success Formula For Your Search Campaign

1. Develop Inspiring Self-Marketing Tools
   a. Personal Value Statements (PVS), commonly known as Elevator Pitches.
   b. Develop a script for emails and phone calls to your network and prospects.
   c. Online profile for LinkedIn and other Social Media channels.
   d. Resume or CV (or even your own 1 or 2 page professional marketing brochure, which includes: a photo, background summary, value you bring, and interests) Remember these tools need to be tailored to each target market, opportunity or company.
   e. Business cards designed to be contact cards (for networking) and cards that show your value (for potential employers).
   f. And possibly, videos, blogs and a website.

2. Establish and Measure Activity Goals
   a. Reach out to at least 10-15 existing contacts or new people every week.
   b. Submit up to 10 online applications (or proposals) per week. Make sure they have been tailored and refined to meet the job or contract requirements.
   c. Personally drop off 5 resumes (or brochures) at businesses per week.
   d. Have coffee or lunch with 2-5 contacts per week, especially if they are quality contacts.

3. Record Feedback and the Next Steps
   a. Keep a detailed online log book, or Contact Relationship Management (CRM) system. It's valuable to record details, ideas and even emotions.
   b. Follow up on agreed upon actions. The idea here is if you've promised to do something for someone else, then do it!

4. Gratitudes
   a. Send handwritten Thank You notes. Personalized emails are better than nothing if you are under time constraints.
   b. Thankfulness and follow through are perhaps the most important activities of all.

5. Prepare for Inquiries and Interviews
   a. Anticipate questions and undergo mock interviews.
   b. See Chapter 5: Interviews and Offers.

RESEARCH SPECIFIC COMPANIES

The mantra here is - Dig and dig more! There are a lot of tools available to help you. It's important to find out as much as you can about companies that align with your personal and professional values, so you can target them in your campaign. Once you have identified a potential company, here are few ways to research them.

COMPANY WEBSITES FOR INFORMATION

Using the Internet, review each prospective company's mission statement, history, products, services and management. This is typically found in the About Us section on their website. Most websites also offer a Career section where you can look for specific openings and apply for positions. The process of online applications has gotten better in recent years. With more advanced websites, you can submit your credentials and answer questions within twenty minutes. Keep in mind that the chance of success of the online application submission process by itself is very low. Typically, several hundred

> ## Ca•reer•ology
>
> *To find good opportunities, you must establish a strong desire for exploration. Embrace this idea, even if you're not comfortable with it at first. The Internet and your network of contacts will be invaluable in the process.*

and sometimes thousands of applications are submitted to companies for a given job. Therefore, be sure to make every effort to do what you can to establish a network within the company before and after submitting your application.

CAREER / JOB FAIRS CAN BE BENEFICIAL

Career fairs can be a great way to get energized, but they can be exhausting at the same time. Unless you are in a high demand job or a company present is on your target list, you should probably consider your attendance as a networking and research task. These are reasons enough to attend, but chances are you will not find a direct opportunity at a career fair.

While at the career fair, learn what you can about the companies present. Get to know several recruiters and find out what jobs are available that peak your interest. Ask questions! Let them explain who they are, why they are there and what makes them stand out in their industry. This is a great opportunity for you to be the boss! Recruiters will be interested in telling you about every open job, even if they are not in your area of interest. Be responsive to their needs and offer to refer qualified candidates from your network to them. This is a goodwill opportunity for you.

Occasionally, we've found recruiters who are present for public relations reasons, research, or to satisfy Equal Employment Opportunity (EEO) requirements, rather than to find qualified candidates. You won't always know. The key to success at career fairs is advance preparation. Research companies in advance and be sure to meet with recruiters in whose company you have a sincere interest. Avoid the rest. Arrive early to mingle with recruiters while they are setting up. Offer to get them coffee or a refreshment! If you find that particular booth is jammed full of candidates, move on and come back later. You do not want to be wasting valuable time waiting in a long line.

LINKEDIN: IT'S RICH WITH INFORMATION

LinkedIn is the leading online professional directory of individuals and companies. It is the focal point of research and in building a preliminary network from which you can subsequently build strong contacts. This powerful tool is growing wildly. In fact, by early 2014, over 93 million Americans and over 259 million worldwide professionals had joined LinkedIn.[55] LinkedIn is now dominating the hiring process. For many recruiters, LinkedIn is the only platform used to find talent. They consider it the best tool for finding both passive and active candidates. LinkedIn allows the passive candidate (one not actively seeking a new job) to be found by a recruiter who can bring opportunities forth, now or in the future. Make sure your profile is current, which includes updating profiles as you change jobs, get promoted, or acquire new expertise or certifications.

LinkedIn, like any other social media site, should be used professionally. It contains profiles of numerous companies. From these company profiles, you can see who within your network you are connected to and begin a professional dialog with them.

ADDITIONAL ONLINE REVIEWS

There are a number of websites where you can read company reviews written by people who are employees and former employees. Keep in mind these reviews are often unmanaged. They may include fictional or disgruntled employees, and therefore, can be subjective and biased. While these websites may serve as a general information tool, don't count on them to be 100% accurate. Do your own research with current or former employees or people who do business with the company or organization. In this way you can obtain more accurate information about the company and its culture.

Glassdoor.com - This website has excellent information for job seekers, including articles, company reviews, ratings, salaries, CEO approval ratings, competitors and more. Job seekers can find and anonymously share company reviews, ratings and salary details.

Vault.com - This is another source of company reviews. Site visitors can read reviews and get the buzz, good and bad for over 10,000 companies. Company overviews are free, which is all you need most of the time.

Hoovers.com - Hoovers has a database of 85 million companies and 100 million professionals. You can see certain details, such as addresses, products, financials, and certain contacts (typically sales and marketing personnel) for free. More detail, such as business insight, industry information and management, is available for purchase.

Reflection

1. Choose 1 or 2 sources from those listed above that can help you in your job search. Start with a basic review and learn to parse through the information.
2. Set a goal to research five to ten companies each week.

"Through hard work, perseverance and a faith in God, you can live your dreams"

DR. BENJAMIN CARSON – SPEAKER, RETIRED NEUROSURGEON

U.S. PRESIDENTIAL CANDIDATE

While implementing your job search campaign, take time to determine if your potential employer's values and practices align with your beliefs and values. Do they provide a product or service you support and appreciate? Do they put equal emphasis on people, profits, and the planet?

Helpful resources for each of these topics include, *What Matters Most - The Power of Living Your Values*, by Hyrum W. Smith[56] with a foreword by Ken Blanchard and *The Triple Bottom Line: What Is It and How Does It Work*, by Timothy F. Slaper, Ph.D. and Tanya J. Hall.[57]

Below is a list of our Top Ten Characteristics to be researched when considering a potential employer.

What Does an Ideal Employer Look Like?
Top Ten Characteristics

1. Inspiring leaders running company – Provide vision and stimulating work. They lead by example.
2. Excellent communicators – Same message to employees/consultants as to customers and shareholders.
3. Triple bottom–line oriented – Equal importance given to people/profit/planet. See glossary for more information.
4. Quality and innovative culture – Not just slogans.
5. Few, if any, 'dumb' rules.
6. Authentic and treats people with respect and dignity.
7. Teamwork focus.
8. Firm but fair with people.
9. Praise given for work well done. They do not micro-manage people.
10. Offers additional pay for performance and other incentives.

THE PASSIVE APPROACH AND FALSE ADVERTISEMENTS

By far, the most successful job or contract search campaigns we've seen are those in which the candidates follow an energetic, proactive approach. Too often many people wait for job postings to appear online or hope their network contacts will share leads for open positions. This passive style is not as effective as following a more aggressive plan of action. Also, it's important for you to realize that even though a job is posted, especially on job boards like careerbuilder.com and monster.com, this does not mean the job is actually available. The job may have been filled and/or an internal candidate is already slated to take the position. This is also true of jobs posted on company websites.

"Yield thou not to adversity, but press on the more bravely."
VIRGIL – ROMAN POET

How are you supposed to know if a job posting you see online is actually available? You won't know until you do some investigation. Don't waste your time and energy applying without finding out more information about the post. This is where your network can help. Track down contacts who can give you some inside information. Do these things before you apply with your cover letter and resume.

> ## Ca•reer•ology
> *Many companies today routinely hire in certain areas of the business while eliminating positions elsewhere.*

Why? Well, first it is true that many jobs are never posted, and our experience suggests that a number of jobs from job sites have already been filled or an internal candidate is already in line for the position. In such a case, the posting likely exists to ensure a company is in legal compliance under U.S. Equal Employment Opportunity (EEO) regulations, or some other corporate reason. Do your research. Ask your network and determine if the job truly exists before applying to a job post!

BUILD A LIST OF TARGET COMPANIES OR ORGANIZATIONS

Sales and marketing professionals are responsible for hunting down prospective customers. Similarly, you won't want to begin your hunt without a target list of companies. You must have several targets on your list. Following this approach, you may find hidden opportunities you could not have imagined. Start with a list of about ten companies.

"Always have your networking 'antennas' up, as you try to get to know as many leaders and employees at each of your targeted companies."
DANA AND PAUL

Follow each company's announcements and check your network for who may be working there or who they know who works there. Ask your contact for a brief meeting over coffee. Remember to ask for their advice first, rather than about specific job opportunities. Asking for advice puts people more at ease and usually better enables them to help you. Referrals from a well reputed connection are always best but also try contacting people within in the company directly as well. Don't be shy. Be bold! Do not exclude a particular company just because there are no openings at the moment or even if they are having layoffs. They could still be hiring elsewhere.

Plan to add three to five new companies or organizations to your target list each week. This will take some effort, but you must do it! This requires you to act and think like an investigative reporter. You will broaden your immediate and future opportunities. About thirty is a practical number of companies to follow and engage with. However, this depends on your situation and your capacity to manage the details of your campaign.

In closing we pray...
Lord, there are many people in our nation who are in need
of a steady job with sufficient wages to care for themselves
and their families.

Help these people remain diligent in their job search. Give
them the confidence they need to succeed and the
perseverance to continue on when they become
discouraged.

Teach me to encourage those seeking employment and to
offer them whatever assistance I can give.
Open the hearts of those responsible for hiring and care of
unemployed people in industry and government so that
they can carry out their work with compassion.

Amen

✝✝✝

Sample Scenario:
Matthew is a 21 year-old, recent college graduate with a degree in art history. Below is his plan of action.

Chapter 4 Key Activities Worksheet
Seek and You Shall Find

A. Research and devise a search campaign.

What?	*Print out and read* A Proven Success Formula *from this chapter. Make a list of target companies and jobs where art history majors are wanted or for which my skills can be transferred*
By When?	*This week*

B. Update Personal Branding material.

What?	*Review current LinkedIn profile and photograph. Give and obtain several recommendations. Create an inspiring Resume*
By When?	*Next week*

C. Goal setting and making contacts.

What?	*Send out 5 LinkedIn invites and attend 2 or 3 Social/business networking sessions*
By When?	*Every week, beginning next week*

D. Thank you notes and fun/reward.

What?	*Send thank you notes to network contacts who helped me with advice or leads*
By When?	*Within 10 days of contact.*

Your Turn: *Completing this form will provide you with valuable insights and action steps.*

Chapter 4 Key Activities Worksheet
Seek and You Shall Find

A. Research and devise a search campaign.

What? _____
_____
_____

By When? _____

B. Update Personal Branding material.

What? _____
_____
_____

By When? _____

C. Goal setting and making contacts.

What? _____
_____
_____

By When? _____

D. Thank you notes and fun/reward.

What? _____
_____
_____

By When? _____

Download additional templates at www.careeringbook.com

Notes & Thoughts

Interview Your Way Into A Heavenly Job!

CHAPTER 5: INTERVIEWS AND OFFERS

Interview Your Way Into a Heavenly Job!

—INTRODUCTION—

Yeah... You did it! You've worked your job or contract search campaign, and you've scheduled your first interview. This excitement is quickly replaced by anxiety when you realize it's time to get prepared to sell yourself to interviewers. Think about the Boy Scouts' credo: Be Prepared. Indeed, self-confidence and meticulous preparation are the keys to your success. You must be ready to tell your story well and project an image that suggests you will fit in and respond effectively to many questions. You do what's needed to get yourself fired up!

We all have our own personal rituals that help us get mentally ready to take on any challenge. Imagine yourself a superhero with a red cape and a big "S" underneath your shirt or blouse. You are there to save the day! Beware of trained or untrained interviewers. They may ask you good, bad or even illegal questions! You won't know until you undergo the process. Every interview will be an opportunity to become better at interviewing. Upon reading this chapter, you will become more familiar with the super skills needed to cultivate more confidence and successfulness in interviewing your way into a heavenly job.

PRACTICE MAKES PERFECT

GO PREPARED!

The biggest mistake in interviewing is not being fully prepared. Like the Boy Scouts' motto, be prepared —for anything. Do your research and practice extensively. This will set you apart from your competition. Think about interviewing as a sales and marketing activity, of yourself. You are your own product and brand. For guidance with this idea, read books and articles on sales/marketing and branding. There are many books on this subject. Masters of the topic include Jeffrey Gitomer, Brian Tracy and Seth Godin, just to name a few.

"By failing to prepare, you are preparing to fail."
BENJAMIN FRANKLIN – U.S. FOUNDING FATHER, AUTHOR, STATESMAN

Everyone has heard the expression, "It's not what you say, but how you say it", and that's crucial during an interview. Additionally, knowing details about the company and information about the interviewers themselves will be very beneficial. Review their LinkedIn profiles, so you can best relate to them during the interview. Your interviewers will feel complimented if your comments are sincere and not excessive.

The underlying purpose of any interview centers on three basic questions from an interviewer's perspective:

Questions Hiring Managers Are Secretly Wondering About You
1. Can you do the job? *2. Will you do the job?* *3. Will you fit into our culture?*

Conveying the answers to these questions, regardless of whether the interviewers actually ask them directly, should be an objective of the interview from a candidate's standpoint. Your interviewers must be satisfied with their conclusions to each question to make an offer to you.

GETTING PREPARED

Your specific preparation data gathering should include:

- **The Company** – products or services, financial condition and outlook, geographical locations, news, culture, reputation, acronyms and buzzwords.
- **The Industry** – trends, key issues, problems, difficulties, strengths, language, acronyms, buzzwords.
- **The Position** – typical duties, skills, trends, salary range.

Also, be sure to prepare/review:

- **About You** - information about yourself – be prepared to succinctly articulate two or three S.T.A.R. statements (Situation/Task/Action/Result) i.e. success essays regarding your major accomplishments.
- **Interesting Statements** - about your strengths, background, interest in the job and organization, commitment to the field, and goals for future.
- **Questions to ask** - the hiring or contracts manager and other interview team members.
- **Ask yourself this?** - "How can I do the job well and contribute to the overall success of the department or unit within this company?" With this question, remember to include your skills that are transferable, such as self-discipline, organizational abilities, and any others that might showcase your strengths.

WHAT SHOULD I WEAR?

Business dress these days varies significantly. While some companies still wear the business uniform of suits/ties for men and dresses for women, many people today dress very casually. It depends upon the organization. Casual dress can include everything from khakis to jeans and athletic shoes. Remember, you have one chance to make a good impression and under-dressing or overdressing could impact the interview. Try to find out how people dress at the potential place of employment and dress one notch better for the interview.

Sample Situation/Task/Action/Results or S.T.A.R. Questions for Interviews and While Networking

S (Situation) – What was the situation?
- I managed a new software release called "OS-8".
- I recognized a lack of volunteers in church's food ministry.

T (Task) – What did I do?
- I wrote code using HTML, supervising two programmers.
- I proposed a detailed plan to church leaders to attract additional volunteers.

A (Action) – How did I do it?
- I developed code and successfully tested in a six month timeframe.
- I designed a recruitment campaign for the ministry.

R (Result) – What happened?
- I released software on time, within budget, and made $5 million in revenue.
- I recruited successfully five new volunteers in six months to the ministry.

Download this template at www.careeringbook.com

MANY TYPES OF INTERVIEWS

Depending upon the company, the traditional live, in-person interview process has changed. For example, some companies will conduct a telephone screen or online assessment before bringing you in for an interview. These are just as important as live, in-person interviews, so you must be prepared. These pre-interviews can be very tough because often you are dealing with a screener and not the main hiring manager. You must understand and be able to relate to this person, regardless of their role.

> ## Ca•reer•ology
>
> *There can be fierce competition for almost every open position. Do your research and practice, practice, practice your interview techniques. And remember - you are interviewing them, too.*

A telephone screen may involve more than one interviewer and can be more difficult than a live interview. Have your facts ready, stay focused and answer the questions succinctly but completely. Do your best to establish rapport with the interviewer(s) as much as reasonably possible. Finding common interests and similarities will help you to relate. Make sure you are in a quiet area with no background distractions and have your resume and answers to questions readily available. During a phone interview be sure to stand up and smile. This will improve your voice inflection. Remember that the sole purpose of the phone interview is to get invited in for a live, in-person interview, assuming you remain interested in the position.

Some companies conduct interviews via video conferencing. This can be more challenging than a phone screen because you must be dressed appropriately, maintain eye contact with the camera and have no distractions in the background. It's all right to use a few gestures and to show your enthusiasm as appropriate. Be ready to start on time and don't show your frustration if the connection fails to work smoothly.

Panel interviews usually involve two or more individuals who alternate asking you questions during the interview. Make eye contact with each panelist and listen carefully to their question. Ask the interviewer to restate their question if it is not stately clearly. Think through the probable reason for the question and be prepared to show some interest in the work problems that might exist. More importantly, if you have encountered their problem(s) before and successfully addressed it, move into your S.T.A.R.

(Situation/Task/Action/Results) statements to demonstrate your proficiency as it relates directly to the interviewer's issue. If the interview is over lunch, be sure to order something simple to eat (not spaghetti) and be considerate of menu prices.

Second or third interviews will likely include higher level decision-makers. In many cases, they may not know much about the details of the position you're applying for. Their job is to render an opinion as to overall fit with the company and to see if there are any red flags about you. They generally prefer jargon-free, summary comments

> **Ca•reer•ology**
>
> *Major Types of Interviews Include:*
> 1. *Phone Screen*
> 2. *Live, In-Person*
> 3. *Panel – Typically Live*
> 4. *Online via Google+, Skype*

rather than elaborate explanations. Keep it simple and always find ways to get them to talk as well.

Professionally trained interviewers will use a technique called behavioral interviewing. These are questions that go beyond the basic facts about your skills and interests. You can identify a behavioral question if it starts with "Tell me about a time when…" or "What was your specific contribution to the major project you've listed in your resume?" This is where you should use your S.T.A.R. statements. What you did, how you did it and what positive results came from your effort may impress the interviewer. Be brief but thorough.

PAUL'S 3RD AND FINAL LAYOFF - THEN THE UNEXPECTED HAPPENED

In his own words: God speaks to us in many ways. The following is a true story by co-author Paul Dean, describing how God spoke to him through the heartfelt actions of his seven-year-old daughter.

Daddy, You Can Come In Now

It was May 2, 2001, and I had just been informed that my job was eliminated. This was my "third and final" layoff episode from Nortel Networks. I called my wife, Barbara, gave her the news and went home. Barbara picked up the kids from school and told them on the way home that Daddy lost his job today, so he is going to be sad when you see him. Our 7 year-old daughter, Andrea, replied, "When I get home, I'll help him find it". Barbara explained what a job was and what it meant to lose a job. Andrea said she understood that, and also what her daddy needed to do in order to get a new job.

When they drove up the driveway, I was in the yard looking at trees and flowers, pondering things. Andrea jumped out of the car and said, "Daddy, don't come in the house yet... I've got something to do!" I usually receive a hug when she comes home, but this time she was on a mission. She darted into the house. Barbara gave me a longer-than-usual hug, and I asked her ... "What's up with Andrea?" She said she was not really sure... but that she explained to her about my job loss and that I would be sad. About 10 minutes later, Andrea opened her bedroom window and yelled, "Ok, Daddy, you can come in now. But, Mommy, you can't come in, this is just for Daddy."

"Applekation"

I went upstairs and Andrea's bedroom door was closed. There was a freshly torn piece of notebook paper taped to the door. In crayon, she had written the words "Knock Before You Enter." I knocked and heard Andrea say, "Come in." She was sitting at her small table and then stood up and said, "Hello, Mr. Dean, please have a seat." She pointed to a small chair, and I crouched down and sat down with her on the other side. She handed me a piece of paper, on which, written with a crayon in her best first grade spelling, was the word Applekation. I soon figured it to be Application, and I played along by writing down my name and address. She acted so professional. She sat with her hands folded and waited. I handed it to her and she said, "Thank you! Now I have three questions you need to answer for this job." She had taken time to write the following three questions on a piece of paper:

1. Do you want to love me and be taking care of me?
2. Do you want to be my daddy, and we will always be together, even in heaven?
3. Do you want to do all the fun things we like to do together?

As I read these questions, I had one of those wonderful emotional moments. I felt good all over. Words really couldn't describe it. Losing my job totally left my mind—I just felt great! I wrote "Yes" next to each question in the space provided and handed it back to her. She read each response and put a check mark next to each one of my answers. She then stood up and said, "Congratulations, Daddy! You have a new job!" I gave her a big hug and said, "Thank You, Dear!" I will take that moment with me until the day I depart this life.

Reflection

Consider what's really important in the big picture. In his case, Paul's young daughter definitely showed him how to put things into perspective!

1. How can Paul's story help you in viewing your career and work-life? What can you learn from his daughter about your own situation?
2. What can help you determine what is really most important to you? Are you living that principle in your daily life? Do you feel that you ignored other values you consider important because of your previous jobs or career choices? List them now.

YOU CAN NOT PRACTICE ENOUGH

You need to ace your interviews to get the job. Many of your competitors will be poorly prepared, while some will be well-prepared, natural presenters, and everything in between. Conducting mock interviews with friends or a career coach and on video will greatly increase the odds of success in your favor. Practice and prepare for the following:

- Both obvious and difficult interview questions. Here are a few thought-provoking ones to get you started.
    o Can you think of a recent problem in which old solutions wouldn't work?
    o Tell me about a past success and a past failure and how you handled each of them.
    o Do you consider yourself a team player? If so, give me a specific example of when you had to demonstrate that in a conflict situation.
- Answering the following basic questions carefully.
    o "Why did you leave your last job?"
    o "How do you feel about your last employer?"

- For additional examples, see *"How to Answer the 31 Most Common Interview Questions"* at www.themuse.com/advice/how-to-answer-the-31-most-common-interview-questions. Write out answers to these questions and you can use them as your pre-testing ground for responding to actual questions an employer may have. To verify your hunches, ask friends, professional or even personal contacts to role play with you and give you feedback on your answers.

- S.T.A.R. – Situation/Task + Action = Result or Outcome Statements. Good S.T.A.R. statements will exemplify your transferable skills, such as leadership, values, and self-discipline.

- Devise a 60 second Elevator Pitch/Personal Value Statement (PVS), tailoring it to higher authorities and those who need to know you.

- Give a firm, but not crushing, hand shake and good eye contact as well as other non-verbal communication gestures. Practice this with both men and women.

- Focus on the questions and the questions behind the questions. Stay on topic and address any hidden needs and wants.

- Make sure you think about responses that answer the questions asked. Be brief and don't take more than a few minutes.

- Bring crisp copies of your Resume, CV or Proposal. Be willing to write a 30, 60, 90 day plan you would implement if hired. This is a bold step, but many employers are looking for action-oriented character traits.

"An effective interview is one where you are well-prepared; you listen carefully, respond appropriately and enthusiastically, and have asked a few smart questions yourself."
DANA AND PAUL

ADDITIONAL INTERVIEW TIPS

1. **Listen Attentively/Active Listening**: By focusing not only on the interviewers' words, but also on their tone and body language, you will be able to pick up subtle cues about their interests and preferences. Formulate

your answers accordingly. This will enable you to establish a personal rapport with the interviewers. If they say something that is inaccurate in your opinion, or a personal opinion you happen to disagree with, let it go. Now is not the time to be argumentative.

2. **Authenticity**. Be confident and show sincere interest and demonstrate how you can add value to the organization.

3. **Use This Cadence**: Always remember to use two or three S.T.A.R. statements (Situation/Task/Action/Results). Quantifiable data is always best.

4. **Focus**. Be prompt. Be concise. Be specific. Be conversational. Be focused. Ask smart questions.

5. **Honesty Actually Works**. Honesty is best. If you do not know the answer to a question, admit it. Sometimes questions are designed to take you to a place where you do not know the answer.

6. **Expect Crazy Questions**. Handle suspect questions (citizenship, age, marital status, number of children). Just answer the question or don't answer the question, but answer the intent instead. Example: "Are you a U.S. citizen?" might be answered, "If you mean am I legally authorized to work for you, then the answer is yes."

7. **Powerful Silence**. Silence is golden—a thoughtful pause will usually work in your favor. Taking a moment, thinking and pausing won't often hurt you during the interview. Remember, this is not a radio or TV show, and so-called dead air can be very useful.

8. **Study Culture**. Each organization or company has its own distinct personality, culture, structure and ways of working. Think in terms of responsibilities, accountabilities and competencies.

9. **Smiling Helps**. Smile appropriately and maintain good eye contact.

10. **A Spirit of Thankfulness**. Thank the interviewer at the end and be sure to communicate your interest in the position, if that is the case. Ask for business cards and what they see as the next steps. Suggest that you would like to become LinkedIn with them. If they consent, be sure to customize your LinkedIn message, referencing the great interview experience you had.

11. **Following up**. No news may not be bad news, but beware. Time will seem to slow down as you wait for an answer. One single day may seem like a week's worth of waiting! Most offers will need to be approved up the

chain of command. If you've heard nothing for more than 10 days or so, send a nice email or try to make contact by voicemail. Express your interest and curiosity as to when they will be making a final decision.

12. **Showing Gratitude.** After the interview, and before you forget, find a private space and write down your impressions, issues and key items discussed. Make sure you send personal Thank You notes to each person you interviewed with, within 48 hours. This response does not have to be email or email only! Get some professional Thank You notes with stamps and mail them. Use this opportunity to reinforce key information, how you can add value and contribute to the organization, and mention any positive afterthoughts. Remind the interviewer of your qualities and accomplishments, but keep it short.

Reflection

1. Think of a person (friend, mentor, or coach) with whom you can put your interviewing skills into practice. Have him or her ask you questions related to your job interests. Record yourself and ask for feedback.

2. Repeat Step 1!

PAUL'S POLLINATED INTERVIEW

In his own words: Below is a true story of an interview Paul had on one unseasonably hot spring day in Durham, North Carolina.

Paul Makes Several Attempts for An Interview

Getting the interview is 'half the battle' in getting the job. Up until working with Nortel, my only other high tech related work was as a temporary contract software tester with IBM. After several applications and referrals from former peers, I finally got an interview for a full-time position. I was ecstatic! On the day of the interview, my anxiety started at daybreak and continued to build. The interview was scheduled for 3:00 pm, and by noon I was a nervous wreck!

Watch Out for That Tree!

Now, in order for you to appreciate this story, you need to understand the weather that day. It was an unseasonably hot day in North Carolina. In fact, it might have been one of those several El Nino-related record highs set throughout the southeast. It was also a peak pollen day - the yellow stuff, pollen/tree sperm that plagues the southeast every spring. It gets everywhere … in your nose, your eyes, and your car, everywhere! You wish and pray for a good rain to wash it away. Well, I was ready to go. Wearing my best dark blue interview suit (No, it was not polyester), I got into my '86 Toyota 4Runner and turned on the air conditioner and discovered it was blowing hot air! Not good! Not a good day to be without AC - 95 degree heat wave, peak pollen and no air conditioning. In my anguished, hot and high anxiety state, I started to back down my driveway and then Wham! I Hit A Tree!!! Oh, great!!! I just then bent my bumper in yet another direction. But I gotta go, must hurry or I'll be late for my interview!

Best Laid Plans

I proceeded to drive 30 minutes to IBM - windows down, sweat beading up on my forehead, capturing any pollen that blew in. Upon entering the IBM lobby, the receptionist took one look at me and stated, "Sir, the washroom is over there behind the elevator." I thanked her and darted to the wash room. I was so happy to be surrounded by cool air; I could feel my pores beginning to close. I looked in the mirror. My face was blood red, my blue suit was covered with a yellowish dusting of pollen, and my white shirt was stuck to my skin. I washed up as best I could, tried to dust off my suit and returned to the lobby. I was still a little sticky, so I went over to a remote side of the lobby and found a floor vent that was blowing a large volume of air, and I stood over it (kinda like Marilyn Monroe did in the movie *The Seven Year Itch*! Boy did that feel good!!) Well, I then went to the interview … gave it my best … but did not get the job. Hmmm … I wonder why!

Reflection

Interviewing by itself is stressful. Distractions are going to happen and you need to be prepared.

1. What can you do to get yourself ready and calm?
2. Visualize having the most successful interview ever!

What shouldn't you do when interviewing? The best way to avoid the most common interview mistakes is to think ahead and decide not to make them. Even the most seasoned professional can get flustered and spoil their chances, so with a little preparation you can avoid these common interview blunders.

Top 10 Interviewing Mistakes
1. Lack of Preparation.
2. Talking Too Much or Too Little.
3. Lack of Poise, Assertiveness or Confidence.
4. Failure to Demonstrate Adequate Business, Industry or Task Acumen/Knowledge.
5. Failure to Highlight Specific, Relevant Short Stories Related to Position or Project (S.T.A.R. – Situation, Task, Actions and Results).
6. Asking Inappropriate, Irrelevant or Untimely Questions.
7. Failure to Relate to Interviewers/Organization – Being Arrogant, Negative or Dishonest.
8. Appearance of Disinterest – By Failing to Express Interest in Job or Contract.
9. Using Poor Diction and Grammar, Lack of Promptness, Focus, Eye Contact or Proper Dress.
10. Cell Phone, Tablet, or Laptop Used Inappropriately.

✛✛✛

"In business as in life, you don't get what you deserve, you get what you negotiate."
CHARLES L. KARRASS, PHD
AUTHOR & PIONEER IN NEGOTIATION STRATEGIES

✛✛✛

PREPARING FOR AND ACCEPTING AN OFFER - NOW WHAT?

Almost everyone who talks about a job offer focuses on the moment the offer is received. In reality, the details of the offer and your negotiations began a lot sooner than you may have thought. As a job seeker, the most important thing to remember is that you will benefit by having an offer-negotiation mindset at the outset of contact. This entails the following, on the next page.

- Realizing that job offer negotiations started the day you connected with an organization.
- Understanding that every communication you have with a prospective employer constitutes negotiations.
- Possibly convincing them to improve the offer in your favor, if they really want you.

In the New World of Work, taking charge of what you can control is important to your success. First, determine the salary range for your occupation in your industry. Search engines and online tools like Glassdoor.com, Payscale.com, Indeed.com and Salary.com will give you a general idea of salary ranges by industry and job. It helps to have an acceptable salary range that you could agree to and then stick to it. Asking the right questions about the position and its scope will help you to determine your salary expectations. Be willing to work within their expected range, and if you feel it is appropriate, shoot for the top of their range scale.

Next, it is important to know that, sometimes, in addition to your pay, other elements of the job can be sweetened, if you are the candidate of choice. You may have fears around asking, but the saying, "nothing ventured, nothing gained" comes into play, and it's unlikely your offer will be threatened when inquiring about a few extras. Some elements of the job offer are often ignored. These should be discussed and sometimes can be negotiated. This includes: vacation days, compensation for training, paid time off (PTO), severance, travel, cell phone expenses, etc. The specifics depend upon the company. Understand the entire offer and don't be afraid to politely ask for a few job-related perks. You will never have as much leverage as you do during the hiring process, other than when you are up for a potential promotion. Offers can be verbal or in writing, not yet often made in a text, a tweet or an Instagram post —but stay tuned!

> # Ca•reer•ology
>
> *Starting salary is often a negotiable item. Be aware of how important it is – a difference of just $5,000 one-time at the start of your career can mean the difference of $784,192 over a lifetime!*
>
> Source:
> *Ask For It* by Linda Babcock and Sara Laschever (2008).

'DUE DILIGENCE'- FOLLOWING UP ON YOUR OFFER

As mentioned earlier, you will want to learn as much as you can about the company's culture and how it matches your character and personality. Similarly, once you receive an offer, you should try to find and contact an existing employee or a former employee for more information. This is another reason to build and maintain a professional network with LinkedIn as a starting tool. When confidentially approached, your network professionals can provide you with information to support your negotiations, but keep in mind, they may be biased. Review comments on Glassdoor.com for other added insight. The key is to ensure that your rapport with both human resources and the hiring manager remains strong. Your ability to communicate and negotiate your value will be noticed and appreciated by the people hiring you.

Finally, do not forget the little things. Without overdoing it, show your sincere excitement upon receiving an offer. Ask for some time to consider the offer, so you can review it. If you have other offers, mildly mention the fact that you do. This takes courage, but it is the most powerful negotiating tool at your disposal! Close with the 'big positives' you see about them.

Dear Lord,

Help me to give of my best today in this interview.

Wrap me in Your loving arms when I feel insecure.

Hold me in Your steady embrace when I feel nervous.

Help me to understand the questions I am asked,

And give answers in a honest and inspired way.

In the interview, I pray You will show me if

this is the right job for me.

I am Your servant, and I seek to do Your

will on this earth.

Lead me in Your paths and guide me into all truth.

I ask all this in the beautiful name of Jesus,

My Savior and friend.

Amen.

Sample Scenario:
Susan is a 46 year-old, stay at home mom who wants to re-enter the workforce. Below is her plan of action.

Chapter 5 Key Activities Worksheet
Interview Your Way into a Heavenly Job!

A. General Preparation.

> What? *Develop and practice 30, 60 and 90 second personal value statements/elevator pitches; update resume and LinkedIn profile*
>
> By When? *This week*

B. Mock Interviewing.

> What? *Prepare 10 questions, develop response and videotape myself*
>
> By When? *Next few days*

C. Dress/wardrobe.

> What? *Find out how employees dress at prospective company. Does my look match the company's culture?*
>
> By When? *A few days before the interview*

D. Thank you notes and fun/reward.

> What? *Send handwritten thank you notes and mail to each person I interviewed with.*
>
> By When? *Within 24 hours of the interview.*

Your Turn: *Completing this form will provide you with valuable insights and action steps.*

Chapter 5 Key Activities Worksheet
Interview Your Way into a Heavenly Job!

A. General Preparation.

What? _____
_____

By When? _____

B. Mock Interviewing.

What? _____
_____

By When? _____

C. Dress/wardrobe.

What? _____
_____

By When? _____

D. Thank you notes and fun/reward.

What? _____
_____

By When? _____

Download additional templates at www.careeringbook.com

Notes & Thoughts

Develop A Free Agent's Mindset

CHAPTER 6: YOUR CAREER JOURNEY

Develop a Free Agent's Mindset

—INTRODUCTION—

In previous times, people typically spent their entire careers with one company. Career management meant taking advantage of company-supported training, benefits, maintaining a good working relationship with the boss, and navigating the culture of the workplace. Today, successful career management includes all of the above, plus providing for most of your own education and training; staying current with developing trends and resources; securing a base of your own employee benefits; and proactive networking intended to help you navigate in multiple workplace cultures, i.e. taking a lifetime lifecycle approach to career management. Today you serve either as an employee, independent contractor, consultant, or entrepreneur, having your own business. Upon reading this chapter, you will learn exactly how to transition from the Old Employee Model to the New Free Agent Model of employment. St. Joseph's resilience against adversity can serve you well and will give you faith in your career journey.

ACCEPTANCE OF 'REALITY'
STEP ONE TOWARD SUCCESSFUL CHANGE

✝✝✝

"The times are bad! The times are troublesome!
This is what humans say. But we are our times. Let us live well and our
times will be good. Such as we are, such are our times."
ST. AUGUSTINE- BISHOP, PHILOSOPHER, THEOLOGIAN

✝✝✝

ST. JOSEPH – A ROLE MODEL FOR CAREER SUCCESS

Pope Pius XII established the *Feast of St. Joseph the Worker* in 1955, which is celebrated on the first of May. In addition to protecting Mary and Jesus, Joseph is believed to have taught Jesus carpentry and can be considered a role model for career success because of his patience, persistence, and hard work. He was also a man of faith who was obedient to whatever God asked of him without knowing the outcome. A number of prayers to Joseph provide direction to us in carrying out our work and a search for new work, including the importance of incorporating and demonstrating:

- Grace, gratitude, and joy
- Purity of intention
- Mindfulness of gifts received from God
- Avoidance of effects of weariness
- Proper handling of difficulties
- Avoidance of bitterness and disappointment

These lessons and guidance from St. Joseph can help you deal with the changing employment landscape.

✝✝✝

"Joseph helps those who are out of work, those deciding on educational or career paths, and those in established occupations. He's a model of all forms of work."[58]

✝✝✝

The New World of Work Lifetime Lifecycle Career Management	
Old Employee Model	**New Free Agent Model**
1. One Company, One Career 2+ Jobs, 1 Company and Career Until Ages 60 to 65.	**1. Portfolio Careers** 10+ Jobs, 5+ Companies and 2+ Careers Throughout Your Life.
2. Single Environment Permanent, Full-Time Employment with Benefits, Education and Training at One Firm.	**2. Variable Environments** Multiple Companies, Industries, Optional Career Paths and Diverse Work Arrangements. Limited Benefits from Companies.
3. Narrow Loyalties Employee and Company Very Loyal to Each Other.	**3. Broad Loyalties** Employee/Consultant's Loyalties Heavily Tied to Profession(s) and Network Contacts. Must Have Plan B Jobs and Occupations as Backups.
4. Limited Commitment Choice to Be Fully Engaged with Company or Not.	**4. Full Commitment** Must act Professionally and Demonstrate Competence in the Business, Technology and Human Dynamics at All Times.
5. Low Security Livelihood Determined Primarily by Boss and the Economy.	**5. More Security** Livelihood Determined Mostly by Achievements, Network and Successful Self-Marketing.
6. Robot Mindset Fit into Company's Mold – Don't Take Risks and Don't Stand Out.	**6. Creative Mindset** Innovations Important – Take Calculated Risks. Build a Strong Identity and Reputation – i.e. Personal Brand.
7. External Self–Worth Personal Identity Tied to Employer – Who You Worked For Was Very Important.	**7. Internal Self–Worth** Personal Identity Tied to Your Life and Career Purpose.

THE OLD EMPLOYEE MODEL - A THING OF THE PAST

Until the 1990's, no organization represented the Old Employee Model better than International Business Machines (IBM). Everyone joining IBM prior to the mid-nineties was essentially guaranteed lifetime employment. As positions became unnecessary, employees were offered opportunities elsewhere within the company, and typically worked at IBM until retirement. Then, in 1993, for the first time in the company's history, a unit of IBM announced layoffs![59]

Other major companies had introduced layoffs previously, but IBM's elimination of their no layoff policy sent a signal to professional employees across the U.S. that lifetime employment with large companies was officially dead. This change impacted people in many ways. Many who were laid off took their talents to other companies. Others went into government, non-profits, or started their own businesses. This period was a fairly robust economic time and most displaced employees were able to transition to new employment without much difficulty.

During the 1990's and 2000's, organizations tended to temporarily suspend hiring following layoffs and established no re-hire policies to avoid feelings of ill will. This is no longer the case. Today it's common for a company to layoff in one segment of its business while hiring in a different segment. Likewise, there is no longer a negative stigma attached to layoffs, so both companies and employees accept what used to be called the revolving door concept.

"You can no longer count on employer–sponsored training to enhance your communications skills or expand your technical know–how"[60]
REID HOFFMAN – CO-FOUNDER OF LINKEDIN
BEN CASNOCHA – WRITER, ENTREPRENEUR

THE NEW FREE AGENT MODEL - THE TREND OF THE FUTURE

Historically, it was not unusual to spend an entire career with a single company and retire at age 65 with a cake celebration, pension and gold watch. If a professional changed employers more than once or twice over twenty years, they were labeled a job hopper! Those who joined and stayed with one company were provided a comprehensive employee benefits package, insurance and pension/savings plans as well as valuable training programs. These programs were designed to provide financial security and professional development. This is no longer standard.

As an employee, you felt very secure in your job, knowing your basic needs and retirement would be met. This is what we and millions of others wanted in our careers. This is no longer the case. With few exceptions, in today's New World of Work, you must take charge of your own destiny—

prepare for different jobs, new employers, and a diverse array of working arrangements.

"Don't put all of your eggs in one basket" is an old saying that applies to workers today. We all understand this responsibility can seem daunting, but embracing the New World of Work with an open mind will provide experiences and fulfillment that were not always available under the Old Employee Model.

An excellent resource for how careers are changing, from an insider's standpoint, includes a white paper by Career Thought Leaders, *Findings of the 2012 Global Career Brainstorming Day: Trends for the Now, the New and the Next in Careers.*[61]

Reflection

Changing jobs, occupations and employment arrangements will enable you to meet people with new and different ideas. Additionally, understanding new technologies and different industries can broaden your mind and help keep you relevant!

1. What are some ways that you can use this type of change to your advantage?
2. How can it help you to grow?

THE IMPORTANCE OF NEW LOYALTIES

As described in the Old Employee Model, many workers assumed lifetime employment with one company and that both company and employee would be loyal to each other. You were family and remained so unless you made major mistakes at work.

An entire book from the 1950's, *The Organization Man,*[62] outlines these principles perhaps more so than any other body of work. For ensuing years and well into the years following the inclusion of females into the workforce, many people were so loyal to the company that they thought of the company as family; taking an outside recruiter's call was near heresy! This is definitely not the case today.

You need to develop a new type of loyalty, including a self-loyalty, to remain relevant. You must expand loyalties within an employer, your community, a church and elsewhere. Do this by regularly participating in groups, blogging, and through volunteering. This gets back to the principle of continually building your network. Your actions are not just for potential job promotion purposes, but also for pure survival reasons because of the transitional nature of the New World of Work.

You will be much better off if you get laid-off, and you have already built goodwill among numerous contacts that can help connect you to new opportunities. Being socially relevant, humanely in touch and individually caring can mean a world of difference if you find yourself at a loss.

Ca•reer•ology

St. Joseph gives us focused strength and a blueprint for persevering with career issues. The actions, virtues, and attitudes he displayed can help us understand how to succeed – despite any obstacle.

COMMIT TO LIFE-LONG LEARNING

Staying current, especially with technology, is crucial to success in the New World of Work. In fact, becoming out-of-date can be a death-sentence to your career. If you don't stay current, your days at your own employer will be numbered, and your success with new employment limited. Remaining up-to-date will also help with interviewing and securing a new job or contract. This effort includes both technical and qualitative skills development. Know how to utilize relevant technology and stay up-to-date with changes in your chosen field. Participate in conferences and review online research/periodicals, listen to TED Talks, and read industry white papers.

"If you stop learning, you stop creating history and become history!"
VADIM KOTELNIKOV – BUSINESS COACH, AUTHOR

YOUR FUTURE SECURITY

In the past, your security was tied directly to your company. Since guaranteed employment is no longer implied, the 'free agent mindset' can help guard against feelings of insecurity. By staying current, adding good people to your network, and self-marketing, you will have more security than ever before.

What do you know about trends affecting your job or career? Are you preparing? Education and training opportunities include certifications online and at local universities as well as at community colleges, covering a wide variety of topics. Commit to a certification program that has become a standard for your type of work. Having certifications behind your name may give your potential employer or your client company a sense of security about hiring you. Enroll in programs that will help you develop your soft skills, such as communications, as well as more common hard skills such as computer training. Make sure to update your online profiles as you complete these various programs.

YOU, INC.

In the New World of Work, you should always have a backup Plan B. Plan B means being prepared for unexpected changes, including abrupt termination of your job or contract. There are a wide range of possible solutions - from having an entirely new job prospect pending, to being up-to-date with a mentor and other key influencers in your network, to having a temporary or permanent plan for self-employment.

Periodically, laid-off individuals come into our Career Network Ministry who are curious about self-employment options. Regardless of whether they pursue traditional employment or an entrepreneurial venture, we encourage them to start thinking of their career as a business. Thinking of your career as a business and adopting a free agent mindset will help you. As a business, you must set objectives, make priorities and stay focused.

As a result of the Great Recession, we have seen more people venture into self-employment. Some have been eager to start their own business while others have been reluctant. In addition to business issues, with self-employment, you must think about employee benefits, for yourself and possibly any employees you hire.

Two highly rated resources for thinking about becoming an entrepreneur include *The Entrepreneur Mind: 100 Essential Beliefs, Characteristics, and Habits of Elite Entrepreneurs*, by Kevin Johnson,[63] and *School for Startups: The Breakthrough Course for Guaranteeing Small Business Success in 90 Days or Less*, by Jim Beach, Chris Hanks, and David Beasley.[64]

Company benefit plans have changed. They are not as comprehensive as they used to be. Now that defined benefit pensions are essentially gone, most companies offer only a 401k or 403b and many do not have a matching provision. Even if you do not pursue the self-employment route, consider supplementing these with your own private pension, life and disability plan outside of any employer. The area of health insurance seems to be shifting with the U.S. Patient Protection/Affordable Care Act. The U.S. Government now guarantees access to health insurance, requiring all citizens to obtain it.

As a free agent, consider negotiating terms and conditions with each new opportunity, as much as possible. Some items are non-negotiable, such as certain employee benefits under ERISA (Employee Retirement Income Security Act) and vacation time if the company is following formal policies and procedures. However, even in a large company, some items, such as pay and perks can be sweetened - if you just ask. As a self-employed consultant vs. an employee, you will not have company provided benefits but more leverage when negotiating your compensation.

> ## Ca•reer•ology
>
> *Some Self-Employment Options*
> 1. *Consulting*
> 2. *Joint Ventures or Other Partnerships*
> 3. *Start and Own a Business*
> 4. *Buy an Existing Business or Franchise*
> 5. *Network Marketing*
> 6. *Direct Sales*
>
> **Disclaimer:** Going solo can be very rewarding or completely fruitless, and everything in between. Consider exploring your options while actively employed. Proceed with knowledge and caution!

The book, *101 Great Ways to Compete in Today's Job Market*[65], by Michele A. Riklan and David Riklan offers a comprehensive guide to job searching and career management. The book is authored by 101 of today's thought leaders and is an easy read, with most segments only three or four pages long. Another book you may have heard of is called *You, Inc., The Art of Selling Yourself*[66] by Harry and Christine C. Beckwith. If you haven't read it, do so! The book is a series of simple, logical lessons on positioning yourself and tactfully promoting yourself inside and outside of a company.

Reflection

Take an honest assessment of yourself and your career characteristics, referring back to the New Free Agent Model in this chapter. What steps can you take to prepare yourself for the New World of Work?

1. Are you living under the Old Employee Model?
2. What characteristics of the New Free Agent Model are you demonstrating?

WHO KNOWS WHAT YOU DO AND HOW WELL YOU DO IT?

For many years the mantra of business success was it's all about 'who you know'. However, when rapid technological advances and globalization came along, it morphed into 'who knows you?' This is an important type of public relations effort you need to execute in managing your career. Nowadays you must strive to ensure that your networks know and follow you. The latest mantra goes like this: 'Who knows who you are, what you do, and how well you do it?' This gets

> ### Ca•reer•ology
> *The more effective you are at creating and presenting a recurring, positive image with enough of the right people, the better your chances of career success.*

us back to the concept of personal branding, which we covered in Chapter 3: Your Career Plan and Personal Brand. Be sure to develop an innovator's mindset about your career so your network can see the value you bring.

YOUR SELF-WORTH - DISCONNECT IT FROM YOUR WORK

In Chapter 2: Why Me? Why Not Me?, we discussed the issue of many professionals' value of self being too tied to work. Other cultures and societies seem better able to decouple work form self. It's critical to do so, for several reasons. First, with the New World of Work and frequent job changes, you are often not in control of your short-term, sometimes long-term destiny. Accept it! Second, unplanned changes can actually be an opportunity for improvement. Embrace changes and try to honor them as gifts.

Glorious St. Joseph,

*Model of all those who are devoted to labor, obtain for me
the grace to work conscientiously, putting the call of duty
above my many sins;*

*To work with thankfulness and joy, considering it an honor
to employ and develop, by means of labor,
the gifts received from God;*

*To work with order, peace, prudence and patience, never
surrendering to weariness or difficulties;*

*To work, above all, with purity of intention, and with
detachment from self, having always death before my eyes
and the account which I must render of time lost, of talents
wasted, of good omitted, of vain complacency
in success so fatal to the work of God.*

*All for Jesus, all for Mary, all after thy example,
O Patriarch Joseph. Such shall be my motto in
life and death.*

Amen.

Sample Scenario:

Randy is a 40 year-old, recently downsized sales and marketing professional who wants to become a consultant. Below is his plan of action.

Chapter 6 Key Activities Worksheet
Developing a Free Agent's Mindset

A. Identify and Evaluate 'Plan B' Job and Career Options.

What? *Make a list of companies and industries that could use my existing skills.*

By When? *January 30*

B. Skills, Training & Certifications.

What? *Take available classes on entrepreneurship/ consulting and talk with consultants who are already established*

By When? *Next few months*

C. Professional Network Building & Maintenance.

What? *Volunteer to lead a group of professionals in a new or existing program (i.e. American Marketing Association, etc.)*

By When? *Investigate and get going ASAP*

D. Family Fun/Rewards.

What? *Take a family hike around a lake or local nature park*

By When? *Once per week*

Your Turn: *Completing this form will provide you with valuable insights and action steps.*

Chapter 6 Key Activities Worksheet
Developing a Free Agent's Mindset

A. Identify and Evaluate 'Plan B' Job and Career Options.

What? _____

_____

_____

_____

By When? _____

B. Skills, Training & Certifications.

What? _____

_____

_____

_____

By When? _____

C. Professional Network Building & Maintenance.

What? _____

_____

_____

_____

By When? _____

D. Family Fun/Rewards.

What? _____

_____

_____

_____

By When? _____

Download additional templates at www.careeringbook.com

Notes & Thoughts

Find and Follow Your Passions

CHAPTER 7: LIFE AND CAREER PURPOSE

Find and Follow Your Passions

—INTRODUCTION—

Whether you are looking for work or gainfully employed, for many workers, happiness, self-esteem and purpose are often tied to their work. Alignment of one's life's purpose, career purpose, values and passions is the ultimate prescription for living a happy and fulfilling life. Achieving this state requires satisfaction with both work and leisure time. Studies show that the majority of U.S. workers, over 100 million people, are dissatisfied with their work and would like to find different employment. It is believed that something needs to change. Employers need to improve the work experience, and workers need to find a means to better appreciate their current situation or find more rewarding employment. The dividing factor lies in finding balance and incorporating choices that inspire workers and employers in mind, body and spirit. Meaningful work can mean a more fulfilling life, and one that is in closer alignment with your purpose as well as God's purpose for your life. In this chapter, you will learn how to ask the questions to bring about clarity of true purpose and the importance of aligning yourself with your passions/interests.

KNOWING YOUR PURPOSE WILL FUEL YOUR PASSION

"Your work is going to fill a large part of your life, and the only way to be truly satisfied is to do what you believe is great work. And the only way to do great work is to love what you do. If you haven't found it yet, keep looking. Don't settle."

STEVE JOBS – CO-FOUNDER OF APPLE INC.

BEGIN THE JOURNEY

For the most part, a major life event, such as divorce, major illness, or job loss forces you to revisit your mission in life. In the Career Network Ministry at St. Andrew, many of the members, who have experienced a recent job loss and are undergoing job transition, find themselves questioning their purpose and passion. If you have felt this way, don't be afraid of these thoughts. By ignoring them, you may jump into an unsatisfying job or career solely because of a perceived or real need for money. Contemplation and prayer will help you focus by starting you on a path that will be more rewarding to you and your family.

NORMA'S STORY – THE BIGGEST BLESSING IN DISGUISE!

In her own words: The following is the story of Norma Quinones, an inspiring mentor of the Career Network Ministry. As the Global Quality Assurance Training and Development Project Manager for a major pharmaceutical company, Norma had to make a major shift from public education to private industry following a job layoff. She explains how hard work, passion, faith, and resilience, all worked in her favor during this stressful time.

Career Advice That Was Painful

Through all my life, I have been focused, driven, determined, and grounded in my faith. Nothing would stop me from accomplishing one of my biggest dreams of becoming highly educated and being a professional/career woman. Not even the gender prejudices and attempts to sabotage my goals that I faced from one of the people I love the most - my father - could hinder me.

128

Norma Works Her Way into the Education Field

I have studied and worked fearlessly all my life. My husband, my children and my faith have sustained me through it all. I hold a bachelor's degree, three master's degrees, multiple certifications, and a doctorate! By 2008, I had worked as a teacher, high school administrator, state director, and as an assistant dean in a prestigious university. I thought I had it all figured out! But, somehow, deep inside me, I knew I needed to change. I was tired and disappointed with the new discourse in the educational field, but what else could I do? I had already worked in education with over 25 years in the profession. I guess God was preparing me for the unimaginable. It was early January when my boss called me to talk, and he laid down the facts. The university was experiencing the biggest financial crisis in its history. Tough decisions for the next academic year were being made. My position was in jeopardy, but no decisions were final. They would come in May.

Her 25-Year Career in Education Abruptly Ends

May came. I had forgotten about the January meeting when my boss invited me to meet again. I really did not have any idea of what was next to come, but I will never forget it. My boss and a HR employee greeted me with a large, yellow manila envelope. They asked me to read it and asked if I had any questions. My position was being terminated due to lack of funds. I was stunned! I asked God how this could happen to me now. What would happen to my children? How would I face my husband? What would I do? So many questions and no answers. I called my husband and children with the unexpected news. I came home and the most beautiful thing happened. My oldest daughter received me with a cake. She said, "Mom, let's celebrate your new future!" And, indeed, a new future had begun.

Norma Struggles with the Loss

During the next few months, I struggled with great sadness, disappointment, anger and fear. I was no longer the focused, driven, and determined woman that I once was. But two things remained—my faith in God and my husband and children's support. It was through prayer that I knew that I did not want to return to education. It was the Holy Spirit's inspiration that led me to where I am now. My husband has always worked in the pharmaceutical industry and most of our friends worked in the same field, too. His field of work has always fascinated me. But how could I make that leap? I had no experience in this field. I applied to multiple positions in the industry, and no one ever called me back.

God's Plan for Norma: Volunteering - Doors Begin to Open

God always has His ways to lead us where He needs us to be. It seemed that the only way to gain experience was either by volunteering, internship, or a practicum. And doors opened one more time for me. This time, it was an unpaid temporary job in a highly reputable biotech company, but with no promises of a regular, full-time position.

However, the opportunity to work for this company would give me the business exposure I long desired. And so I did. I fell in love with the company the moment I walked through its doors. I knew I belonged there. One thing led to another. I worked for eight months without pay, but I learned new things and met new people. By Christmas, I was offered a twelve month contract and by June I was offered a regular, full-time position. Since then I have been promoted twice, and I currently lead global programs for the company. It has been now almost five years since I was laid off, but by the Grace of God, I have learned never to quit nor be weary. I learned that, with faith, family support, dedication, and determination, we can rise to levels of achievement that we never imagined we could. Being laid off has been one of my biggest blessings in disguise!

Reflection

1. What emotions, points, and realizations in Norma's story can you relate to?
2. How does her initial response to hearing about her layoff match where she is today?
3. What can you take away from her daughter's response?

"Be not deceived; God is not mocked: for whatsoever a man soweth, that shall he also reap."
GALATIANS 6:7

ARE YOU LIVING YOUR PURPOSE?

Do you love what you do? Be honest with yourself. Do you really love what you do? Are you passionate about something? Do you have a dream, a wish, a feeling that if all were different, you'd be doing something else? This is about you. Understand that only you can define what drives you. What is the driving force inside you? Only you can uncover it, and only you can decide whether or not to act upon it. Until you do, you will always have a nagging feeling that will keep you looking for something until you know you've found it.

"What lies behind us and what lies before us are tiny matters compared to what lies within us."
RALPH WALDO EMERSON – AMERICAN ESSAYIST AND POET

When asked about having a purpose, many people answer this question from a superficial point of view – "I am an accountant; I am an engineer; I am a strategy consultant, etc." This type of explanation is typical for society, thinking that it's all right that happiness and self-esteem is tied to one's work. For the most part, people identify with their title and position more than with a spiritual

> ### Ca•reer•ology
> *Your perspective determines your ability to manage and handle the level of importance and influence that both work and career occupy in your life.*

sense of who they are and the work they do. However, the problem is that actually, the center of your life suddenly becomes a crisis point when challenged with losing this part of your identity. When faced with a job loss, layoff or unemployment, they face an experience that challenges their self-esteem, self-value and sense of worth, not to mention their future livelihood and quality of life.

It's normal to grieve the loss of a job and work relationships, but don't get lost in the grief. Use every tool available to you to emerge from any grief, including your friends/family and other support systems, such as a career ministry. Make it your mission to identify and find your purpose. This will ignite your passions, helping to align your choices and values to your work.

✝✝✝

"There's no greater thing you can do with your life than follow your passions – in a way that serves the world and you."

SIR RICHARD BRANSON – ENGLISH BUSINESS INVESTOR

FOUNDER OF THE VIRGIN GROUP

✝✝✝

IDENTIFYING YOUR PURPOSE

Ideally, having a purpose should transcend your physical life; thus, it should go beyond the day-to-day responsibilities of making a living. "Having clarity of purpose can be a powerful tool in guiding your thinking, choices and behaviors as you navigate through life – both personally and professionally," according to Executive Coach Bill Spreitzer.

Numerous studies show that many professional workers' measurement of self or purpose is determined by their job, at least when measured by job loss.[67] This is especially true for Baby Boomers. While your job or occupation may be an important part of your life, it should not be as important as other aspects of your life, such as family and your faith. A first-hand account was given in Paul's story of his layoff and his young daughter's response to that distress in Chapter 5: Interviews and Offers.

How do you put your career and occupation into proper perspective? This requires different viewpoints and the answer depends on what you value. For instance, if you make security and financial gain the driving force for your choices, you will undoubtedly have a harder time handling and managing an unforeseen layoff, especially if you had counted on it for a retirement, the purchase of a home, or that planned dream vacation. There is no single answer to this question, except how you view yourself, in light of life's journey. That will significantly contribute to how you manage the situation. If you see yourself as a God-centered individual, made in the image and wholeness of God, and that He has a plan, your reaction may be different than that of someone who does not believe or put faith in anything he or she cannot see.

Reflection

Some soul-searching questions you might ask yourself include:

1. What are you sowing by your efforts, your interests, your intentions, your focus and your labor?

132

2. Is it something that supports life, people, society, or a cause? Is it something that is helping create more dissent, dismay, disappointment and demise?
3. What part of the New World of Work are you creating?

Brainstorming Questions
Identify Your Passions!

1. Consider how you define your passion as it relates to your life, work, hobbies, and dreams. Write it down. You may want to even draw pictures.
2. What makes you feel most alive?
    – Work accomplishments
    – Family fun
    – Individual sports, hobbies, etc.
3. List your key interests.

    _____, _____,

    _____,

4. Are you pursuing these interests in your life or career?
    If not, what is preventing you? Note: Go deep and think about how you feel.
5. Are you living a life that is consistent with your core values?
6. If you could make changes to your life and career that would provide you with the most benefit to yourself and others?
    – Mentoring others
    – Achieving big goals
    – Family involvement, etc.

Deeper questions to help uncover your passions:
1. What social injustices in the broader world disturbs you most or breaks your heart?
2. Do you think that past sufferings have brought you closer to your passions and to God and/or His mission for your life?

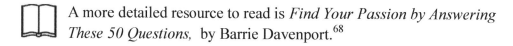

A more detailed resource to read is *Find Your Passion by Answering These 50 Questions,* by Barrie Davenport.[68]

✠✠✠

"If you can't figure out your purpose, figure out your passion. For your passion will lead you right into your purpose."
BISHOP T.D. JAKES – CHIEF PASTOR OF THE POTTER'S HOUSE, AUTHOR

✠✠✠

Remarkably, most Americans are seemingly unhappy with their work. A Gallup poll found that only 30% of American workers are "engaged or inspired" by their work, and 70% do not feel passionate about their job.[69]

> ## Ca•reer•ology
> *By most accounts, life is too short and work is too long not to find passion in how you spend your time.*

Other surveys reinforce the Gallup poll to a large extent, demonstrating that, with a workforce of around 150 million, between 60 million and 105 million workers in America are not passionate about their job. These are tragic statistics!

THE BEST TIME TO BEGIN A CHANGE IS NOW!

It is important to be passionate about your life, work and the energy you are exchanging for the commodity of money. Find something worthwhile you can get excited about, either at your present employer or elsewhere if necessary. After all, this is probably the only human life you will have, so take charge of making the most of it!

If finding passion is difficult in your current situation, consider building a master plan for change. Ask yourself, "How am I spending my time and energy?" You are the creator of the actions that can produce better results. This will happen when you step out of your comfort zone and become aligned with your inner voice. Don't be hyper-focused on your personal "To Do Lists", cell phones and computers. Remember to have productive face-to-face communication, which can lead to conversations that can help you in identifying your passions and purpose.

An excellent source of work around this subject of finding true purpose and meaning in life can be found in Matthew Kelly's book, *The Rhythm of Life: Living Every Day with Passion and Purpose.*[70] Through his work, Kelly helps you discover your legitimate needs, deepest desires, and unique talents. He introduces you to 'the-best-version-of-yourself' concept and helps lead you to a life filled with passion and purpose.

Reflection

If you really do not love what you're doing, when would be the best time to address your situation? Go introspectively by asking yourself the following questions.

1. Do I wake up with an inner feeling of optimism and satisfaction toward my life and career?
2. Am I inspired by what lies ahead? Am I unhappy and dissatisfied, wishing there were another way?
3. What we are is God's gift to us. What we make of ourselves is our gift to God.

"...when you were just a dream, your purpose had already been assigned. Purposefully created, and created for a purpose, you are here at this very moment to become the-best–version–of–yourself."
MATTHEW KELLY – AUTHOR, SPEAKER, CONSULTANT

YOUR ULTIMATE MISSION

In executing your mission in life, having clarity of purpose is essential. Clarity of purpose means being in service to something or someone bigger than yourself. This can be a powerful tool in guiding your thinking, choices and behaviors as you navigate through life—both personally and professionally. Choosing a spouse, career, job or organization to work for should ideally be aligned with your life's purpose. What if we all adopted Kelly's idea of being 'the-best-version-of-ourselves', as our ultimate mission? And what if we sought out this ultimate mission in our daily lives?

The diagram on the next page illustrates the association and interaction of how the alignment of values, passions and life purpose support and promote the ultimate mission of being 'the-best-version-of-yourself'.

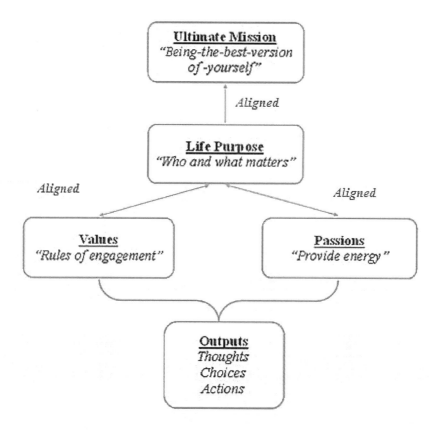

Life Purpose can be described as who and what matters most to you. Your values are your every day rules of engagement. Your passions are the energy/fuel that provides and supports your action. Purpose and passion are linked. Identifying your passions can shed some powerful light as to your purpose. Purpose ignites your passions. Passions provide the fuel for you to further pursue, more of your purpose on a deeper level.

Ca•reer•ology

Passion expresses your uniquely gifted talents, messages and 'inter- knowing' that only you and you alone can bring to realization.

DEVELOPING YOUR PASSION

Having passion inspires your choices and your willingness to persevere when roadblocks get in the way. It defines the energy and zeal you have to pursue the areas of interest that call you, whether they are in sports, movies, art, literature, religion, spirit, music, or philosophy.

When connected to purpose, passion supports you to energetically and deliberately engage in your purpose. It inspires the desire you have to contribute, design, generate or create. It inspires you to continue moving in the direction of your dreams. It also brings about a mission and vision that is unique to you. It is a calling that comes from deep within your spirit. It is the mark that God left on you.

You need to look within yourself. Seeing yourself from an outsider's point of view can give you a window in light of your purpose. Consider, if you were able to see yourself from another's perspective, would that person say you are living your purpose?

Values transcend occupation, position, awards, income, promotions, benefits and long-term job security. Work to align your values and keep the purpose and passion perspective alive within you always.

"Where your talents and the needs of the world cross –
there lies your calling."
ARISTOTLE – GREEK PHILOSOPHER

You must invest time and reflection to uncover the feelings that matter and inspire you, in one way or another. Many individuals, both male and female, respond differently when being asked to define their feelings. You must look at your life and point out the areas, experiences, and opportunities that stand out in your mind and that have touched you emotionally. Only then will you be able to enter the area where your hidden gift lies, awaiting to be uncovered.

"We are not human beings having a spiritual experience; we are spiritual
beings having a human experience."
PIERRE TEILHARD DE CHARDIN – FRENCH PHILOSOPHER, AUTHOR

✟✟✟

WHY AM I ON EARTH?

Most people do not spend much, if any, time on this all-important question – What is my overall purpose? And even if you have spent time on this question, the answer may be still a work-in-progress. Ultimately, answering this question can give clarity to your individual aspirations and daily actions. Sandra Bueno, Personal Performance Coach says, "Figuring out what our intellectual gifts and spiritual capacities are leads us into uncovering a path for our lives where our spirit can live out its physical being." By the same token, your spirit will channel its purpose through your physical body and your work, but only if you allow it to.

YOUR PASSION AND PURPOSE CAN CHANGE THE WORLD

Although your job is important, work is primarily a means to certain ends. The important issues are deepening your relationships, cultivating God's plans for you, and supporting each other. For Catholics, this is where we can remember the Great Commission; we are called to be the body of Christ and to do God's will on this earth. In the process, God will bless our efforts. As believers, we can use the Seven Gifts of the Holy Spirit: Wisdom, Understanding, Right Judgment, Courage, Knowledge, Reverence and Wonder to guide us on a plan that honors God and where we will be instruments of His Grace.

We can also be guided by the Fruit of the Holy Spirit: Charity, Joy, Peace, Patience, Kindness, Goodness, Generosity, Gentleness (or Humility), Faithfulness, Modesty, and Self-Control to help us align with our values in choosing employers and companies. Balancing the physical with the spiritual is the goal that will enable us to keep our lives and decisions in check.

"Darkness cannot drive out darkness; only light can do that.
Hate cannot drive out hate; only love can do that."
MARTIN LUTHER KING, JR. – PASTOR AND CIVIL RIGHTS LEADER

FINAL THOUGHTS

You have an enormous opportunity to pursue and do work that is meaningful, fulfilling, and rewarding through passion and purpose. Believe in yourself and your God-given abilities, perhaps even becoming a change agent in the world.

As with life and career management, our belief is that you must not sit back and expect someone else to solve your problems. Instead, the solution lies within you - and us - working together and helping each other. Remembering what is most important, even more so than any work, our love of God, our love of family, and the ability to practice extraordinary forgiveness. These are perhaps the most powerful of the most potent principles that we can employ in making the world a better place for ourselves and for future generations. Everything begins and ends with love, in accordance with God's will. May we learn how to see this in our everyday world, through our daily activities, the people we meet, and the work we allow ourselves to do.

JOIN US IN SUPPORTING THE CAREERING MOVEMENT!

TELL US YOUR STORY

You are not alone. We are building a community of like-minded souls, who are supportive of The Careering Movement, where we can support each other using the Careering model. Go here and tell us your story.

www.careeringbook.com or
www.facebook.com/Careeringbook

✠✠✠

"Your Career Is Our Cause!"

May God bless you and your loved ones
DANA AND PAUL

✠✠✠

Sample Scenario:
Debbie is a very successful business owner who recently sold her practice for millions. Below is her plan of action.

Chapter 7 Key Activities Worksheet
Find and Follow Your Passions

A. Redefining your next role.

What?   *Decide whether to launch or join a new for-profit or non-profit venture, and/or various volunteer or family activities*

By When?   *Next six months*

B. Personal development and well-being.

What?   *Step-up exercise program and enroll in a personal development course (spiritual, purpose, philosophy, legacy, etc.)*

By When?   *Next six months*

C. Family and Giving Back/Paying it Forward.

What?   *Consider teaching at a local community college or SCORE to help business owners*

By When?   *Next six months*

D. Legacy work.

What?   *Refer to section titled,* Your Ultimate Mission, *and review the diagram to identify my life and career roadmap*

By When?   *Work on a plan and have plan built within six months*

Your Turn: *Completing this form will provide you with valuable insights and action steps.*

Chapter 7 Key Activities Worksheet
Find and Follow Your Passions

A. Redefining your next role.

What? _____
_____
_____
_____

By When? _____

B. Personal development and well-being.

What? _____
_____
_____
_____

By When? _____

C. Family and Giving Back/Paying it Forward.

What? _____
_____
_____

By When? _____

D. Legacy work.

What? _____
_____
_____
_____

By When? _____

Download additional templates at www.careeringbook.com

141

In closing we pray.

Most Holy Spirit, continue to enlighten our hearts
with Your wisdom and council.

Fill us with the love of God.

Teach us to encourage everyone to remain diligent and proactive in
their career life and journey in becoming the best version of
themselves.

Give us the confidence we need to succeed and
the perseverance to continue on when we become discouraged.

Help us in the spirit and understanding that "St Joseph was a man
of faith, obedient to whatever God asked of him without knowing
the outcome," that we, too, will faithfully follow whatever plan God
has for us.

Amen
✝✝✝

APPENDIX I
HOW TO HELP BLUE COLLAR, SERVICE, AND SKILLED TRADES WORKERS

THE FOUNDATION OF OUR COUNTRY'S ECONOMY

A TRUE STORY
"The Ukrainian owner of the North Carolina operations of chicken processor Townsend plans to close all the company's facilities by October and lay off more than a thousand workers in Siler City and Mocksville. The move, which will also terminate contracts with about 200 chicken farmers in four counties, brings an abrupt end to an investment that was viewed as a lifeline for the state's poultry industry."
    – News and Observer, Raleigh NC July 30, 2011

      This story is one of the recurring themes we've all heard about 'Workplace America' for many years. Mass layoffs at lumber mills, textile mills, and manufacturing plant after manufacturing plant have taken their toll on individuals and families for a long time. Yet, often, such layoffs are met with denial and lack of appropriate support from local government agencies—and even churches—who could, and arguably should, provide both practical and spiritual help.

      Very often, blue collar, service, and skilled trades' workers are trained and experienced in very constricted jobs. Therefore, unless they have developed secondary skills through experience or community college courses, they are frequently and woefully unprepared for a transition that re-employment often entails. Few have a Plan B and many do not have the financial resources or cash reserves to provide for extended unemployment.

WHAT CAN YOU DO TO HELP?
There are a number of steps that you can take to help the blue collar, service, and skilled trades brothers and sisters when unemployment strikes (and preferably before unemployment strikes). We believe we can each do our part

to respect the dignity of work and the worker, through our hiring and employment practices, through advocacy for better working conditions, fair wages, for an end to unjust discrimination and through our daily purchase decisions. As fully-engaged, motivated individuals, we can build and maintain a much better society within the United States of America!

Here are some practical ideas:

1. *Establish a Jobs/Career Ministry* that includes a group, especially for blue collar, service, and skilled trade workers, at your church.
2. *Remind and Encourage* workers to take advantage of state or regional career services that provide job search, resume, networking skills, etc.
3. *Promote the value of Training and Retraining* that might be available at the nearest community college.
4. *Become a mentor* to help individuals and families with employment issues:
   a. Practical and spiritual support—empathy, financial guidance, and encouragement
   b. Job leads and connections for networking
   c. Employment and self-employment brainstorming options

"By taking an active role in helping blue collar, service, and skilled trades' brothers and sisters in your community with employment issues, you will be performing the will of God in the spirit of a loving neighbor while maintaining the overall social-economic health of your community."
DANA AND PAUL

APPENDIX II
HOW TO START A JOBS AND CAREER MINISTRY

SANCTIFYING THE DIGNITY OF WORK

Work constitutes a foundation for the formation of family life, which is a natural right and something the human person is called to do. It must be remembered and affirmed that the family constitutes one of the most important vehicles for shaping the social and ethical order of human work. The family is simultaneously a community made possible by work and the first school of work, within the home, for every person.[71] Unemployment and under-employment almost always wounds an individual's dignity and threatens the stability of his/her life. Besides the harm done personally, it also impacts the family.

Based on numerous reports, as of June 2014, a reasonable estimate of both unemployed and under-employed citizens includes 35 to 40 million Americans. In addition, today professional workers are changing employers every 4.6 years, on average. A growing byproduct of these changes is the rise of the 'contingent workforce', with almost 1 in 4 employed Americans now working on a contractual, freelance, temporary, and part-time or project basis.

"Having a Jobs and Career Ministry helps to build fellowship, spiritual growth, and security among the entire church community."
DANA AND PAUL

The reality is that these statistics affect all communities, including your own. For much of America, a lack of financial security has significantly contributed to too many of our problems, including higher rates of crime, domestic violence, excessive anxiety, illness, divorce, and even suicide. We believe that each and every church has an opportunity, if not an obligation, to help bring solutions and support to people. By establishing a Jobs and Career Ministry at your church, you can help participants take ownership of their job search and career or business development issues. Gainfully employed workers and successful business owners contribute to a more prosperous environment, which benefits the community at large, as well as the church. Additionally, improved financial security helps to lessen the social problems associated with unemployment and under-employment.

STEPS IN ESTABLISHING A JOBS

AND CAREER MINISTRY

1. As a leader or member who recognizes the need, request a meeting with church leadership.
    a. State the value of having a Jobs/Career Ministry
    b. Seek support – facilities, promotions, Ministry leadership, and budget (if applicable)
    c. Decide upon action steps for implementation i.e. deadlines, structure, launch date, etc.
2. After obtaining leadership support, decide upon a format for the Ministry. This could be anything as simple as coffee and donuts to a formal curriculum.
    a. Consider available resources – people and budget
    b. Size of Ministry can be determined by the need within the community and the church
    c. Establish meeting agendas and guidelines for participation
3. Publicize the Jobs/Career Ministry through announcements, bulletins, church's website, and social media.
    a. Design a customized communications plan
    b. Ensure that all church communications are consistent with the goals of the Ministry
    c. Emphasize that your Ministry can be of benefit to everyone – i.e. unemployed, under-employed and even actively employed. Retirees can also contribute their work experiences and, in some cases, contacts
    d. Consider promoting your Ministry as a community outreach program

A Career Ministry can be as simple as coffee and donuts after a Sunday service or a weekly meeting with an agenda. Below is a sample agenda that we use at our bi-weekly meetings.

Career Network Ministry at St. Andrews
The Apostle Catholic Church, Apex NC
Sample Agenda

1. Welcome and introduction of guest speaker (an actively employed professional).

2. Personal value statements 'Elevator Pitches' – 90 seconds each, including targeted companies, industries, or client types.

3. Presentation by guest speaker – 30 to 45 minutes.

4. Job search activities and accomplishments since last meeting.

5. Barriers and disappointments since last meeting.

6. Successes and accomplishments since last meeting.

7. Activities planned for next week.

8. Rewards and family fun planned for next week.

9. Closing prayer.

APPENDIX III

FOSTERING DIGNITY AND ENGAGEMENT IN THE WORKPLACE

BRING WIDESPREAD PURPOSE AND PASSION TO YOUR ORGANIZATION

This Appendix is designed to be only an overview, not an extensive plan, for improving engagement at your organization. The answers come from combining the elements of personal responsibility and the Catholic doctrine of dignity of work, each of which have been covered throughout this book. Personal responsibility means, as an employee, taking the time and making an effort to develop a positive mindset, improving upon work habits, and taking more ownership of one's career.

Dignity of work speaks to employers in ways that can result in attracting and retaining quality employees/contractors and consequently, receiving the benefits of a more engaged workforce.

"The dignity and performance of human beings is maximized when employees are given meaningful work where they can see a direct connection between their efforts and the organization's overall goal; when personal accountability exists where the employee feels that what he or she does matters; and when supervisors and leaders treat people with respect in order to achieve a positive climate of dignity in organizations."
- CLIF BOUTELLE, SOCIETY FOR INDUSTRIAL AND ORGANIZATIONAL PSYCHOLOGY

Remarkably, most Americans are seemingly unhappy with their work. A Gallup poll found that only 30% of American workers are "engaged or inspired" by their work.[72] That means 70% do not feel passionate about their job. Other surveys reinforce the Gallup poll, demonstrating that with a workforce of around 150 million, between 60 million and 105 million workers in America are not passionate about their job or employer.

These are startling statistics and translate into increased costs and frustrations for both employers and employees. Poor engagement and low morale mean that performance and profit suffer. A study by HR research and advisory firm McLean & Company found that disengaged employees cost organizations an average of $3,400 a year for every $10,000 in annual salary. This also means, lost productivity and innovative ideas that could propel organizations and revenues.[73] For employees, and subsequently their loved ones, this can often result in negativity, subpar earnings, and a loss of fulfillment and purpose.

"Engaged organizations grew profits as much as three times faster than their competitors. Earnings per share growth of 89 organizations found that the growth rate of organizations with engagement scores in the top quartile was 2.6 times higher than organizations with below-average engagement scores".
- STAN PHELPS, AUTHOR AND SPEAKER, AT 9" MARKETING

Finally, the Corporate Leadership Council reports that highly engaged organizations have the potential to reduce staff turnover by 87% and improve performance by 20%.[74]

The main categories that support the fostering of increased personal responsibility and "drive" dignity and engagement at work are listed below.

Three Drivers of Dignity and Engagement	
1. Fostering a healthy organizational culture	Establishes an organization's positive atmosphere
2. Cultivating healthy business leadership practices	Creates an organization's character
3. Encouraging healthy individual development	Affects personal and team performance and results

Driver #1: A Healthy Organizational Culture means creating clear "visuals" or perceptions so that those working within the organization can understand, see and experience the values, history, demographics, principles, rewards, and communications that create the "atmosphere" of the organization. This also includes a shared set of assumptions and beliefs, which govern how those working within the organization behave. These shared values have a strong influence on those working within the organization and dictate how they dress, act, show-up for and perform their jobs.

Effective -
- Developing and maintaining an organizational culture where employees and contractors are:
  o treated with dignity and respect
  o sincerely recognized for excellent performance
  o work and act together as a high-performance team
  o managed firmly and fairly
- Leadership offers transparency and clearly communicates with employees and contractors.

Ineffective
- Emotional needs and important outside interests of the employee are not taken into consideration
- Backstabbing, gossip, unhealthy competition and negativity are cultivated and pervasive within certain business units or departments
- Processes and administrative paperwork become more important than actual products and services

Cultivating Healthy Organizational Culture using a Careering Paradigm
- Fostering and supporting innovation and collaboration throughout the organization
- Leadership in supporting a higher purpose or vision and finding ways of making it meaningful to employees and contractors
- Inspiring leaders who exhibit great communications skills, online and live, who are successful and fair-minded achievers

Driver #2: Healthy Business Leadership Practices include written and unwritten policies that result in actions and behaviors by managers and employees that contribute significantly to the organization's success, affecting not only the entire workforce – employees and contractors both on-site and remote – but others such as customers, stockholders, and other stakeholders.

Effective
- Fostering an environment where customers, employees and contractors are treated with respect and care
- Supporting organizational leadership and employees in living out the company's vision and values
- Clearly written policies and procedures directing employees and serving customers
- Cultivating an environment of high integrity where management and employees are well trained in utilizing practices - "everyone walks the talk"
- Fostering an environment of customer experience excellence
- Listening to customer and employee input, creating an atmosphere where engagement is valued

Ineffective -
- Poor product or customer service practices
- Lack of vision and or values or disregard by leaders of company's vision and values through their day-to-day actions
- Poorly thought-out, lengthy policies and procedures
- Ineffective hiring and human relations activities
- An environment of decreased integrity where management and employees do not follow company policies and procedures

Cultivating healthy business leadership practices using a Careering paradigm
- Establishing guidelines, policies and procedures that support the incorporation of gainful employment, diversity, social media, trainings and customer engagement for organizational good
- Incorporating dignity of work action steps throughout the organization

- Establishing programs supportive of process, product and service innovation

Driver #3: Healthy Individual Development means implementing an authentic program to boost the expertise and skills of employees, thereby supporting their personal and career growth. This goes beyond just training for promotions, and lies within helping employees in fostering interpersonal and relationship building skills in an environment where learning is not just modeled, but encouraged for all levels of the organization.

Employees are whole people who rarely exist separately from their personal lives. Some may be able to compartmentalize incidences of personal difficulties, such as chronic illness, divorce or death of a loved one, but more often than not performance and engagement are severally impacted. An organization depends on the expertise and engagement of its employees to produce and maintain business.

The nature of the work and the person's match or mismatch also affects engagement. It's important to fully understand and determine where a person may best fit, in order to optimize and achieve good results. Finally, the boss and associated peers have a huge impact on a worker's attitude and outlook, perhaps more than any other factor.

It is important to keep in mind the interconnectivity of cultivating healthy individual development of employees within employer controlled environments. Employees can only do this in an environment where the employer fosters good attitudes and therefore better productivity and engagement.

Effective -
Individual employees are committed to:
- optimism with a mindset of growth and development
- whole body in life - health and wellness
- curiosity and lifelong learning
- maintaining "positive self-talk"
- enhancing productivity and appropriate use of social media

Ineffective -

- Being so driven or directed toward immediate profits that employees forget or do not value the long term health and well-being of the organization
- Little regard for their own mental or physical health
- Disengagement from supporting the company's mission and vision
- Discouragement of lifelong learning

Cultivating Healthy Individual Development using a Careering Paradigm

- Employer fosters a resilience-focused environment where failures from good faith and well-conceived efforts are viewed as an opportunity for learning and perhaps a stepping stone for future accomplishments
- Employer encourages curiosity, learning, innovation, team play, integrity, mental and physical health, and pride in work and organization
- Employees exhibit both soft skills of interaction and positive mindset along with traditional hard skills of knowledge and practices of the job itself

By addressing all three drivers, Organizational Culture, Business Leadership Practices, and Individual Development you will be on your way to improving dignity and thereby improving engagement of your employees. It is the right thing to do for your employees/contractors, customers/clients, your organization and in fact, your country. The rewards are unlimited!

GLOSSARY

Active candidate – a term used to describe a person who is activity-engaged and participating in the act of seeking new employment.

Adult internship – a type of entry level or transitional job that could serve as a vital step in gaining the experience and contacts needed to make a career change or get back into the workforce after a break.

Altruism – the quality of unselfish concern for the welfare of others.

American Dream - a national ethos of the United States, a set of ideals in which freedom includes the opportunity for prosperity and success, and an upward social mobility for the family and children, achieved through hard work in a society with few barriers.

Baby Boomers (Boomers) – 76 million Americans who were born between the years 1946 and 1964 or Post World War II demographic.

Behavioral interviewing – a technique used by employers to learn about your past behavior in particular situations. Past behavior is a better predictor of future behavior than is speculation (on your part) about how you would act in a hypothetical future situation.

Blog – an article that allows users to reflect, share opinions, and discuss various topics in the form of an online journal while readers may comment on posts.

Blue collar worker – a member of the working class who typically performs manual labor and earns an hourly wage.

Bots – robotic software applications that run automated tasks over the Internet. The most ubiquitous bots are the programs also called spiders or crawlers, which access websites and gather their content for search engine indexes.

Brainstorming – a group or individual creativity technique by which efforts are made to find a conclusion for a specific problem by gathering a list of ideas spontaneously contributed by its member.

Careerology – a term utilized in this book to generalize the study of developing and managing specific aspects of one's career and life purpose.

Careering – a term used to describe the journey, experiences, and actions one can take to successfully navigate their career life.

Career assets – a term used to describe the bank of tools an individual has acquired over the course of his/her career. These can be any combination of hard skills (analytical, financial, computer, etc.) and/or soft skills (working with others, interpersonal skills, etc.).

Career Fair – a scheduled event where employers offer information and answer questions about their organization in recruiting new employees.

Company profile – business details such as company name, address, age, business structure and information about its products or services.

Company review – an evaluation or critique of a company by a 3rd party that can cover anything from the quality of service/product, to work environment, financials, market position and outlook.

Contingent workforce – a provisional group of workers who work for an organization on a non-permanent basis, also known as freelancers, independent professionals, temporary contract workers, independent contractors or consultants.

Consultant – a person whose occupation is to be consulted for their expertise, advice, or help in an area or specialty. Typically paid by 1099, rather than W2.

Contractual worker– see Contingent workforce.

Curriculum Vitae (CV) – a detailed written account of one's life comprising one's education, accomplishments, work experience, publications, etc.; especially, one used to apply for a job.

Defined Benefit Pension Plan – a defined benefit pension plan is a type of pension plan in which an employer/sponsor promises a specified monthly benefit on retirement that is predetermined by a formula based on the employee's earnings history, tenure of service and age, rather than depending directly on individual investment returns.

Demographic group – a group of people who are selected based on fitting some set of human or geographical characteristics.

Digital divide – a term used to describe the contradiction of more and more connections with other people via the Internet but with less depth due to less face-to-face interaction.

Dignity of work – a term used in catholic social teaching. Work is an obligation under God and a right in fulfilling our personal role in humanity. Dignity of work encompasses a person's sense of pride, self-worth and security, as well as certain rights of workers to fair treatment by employers, ensuring that people are respected and valued.

Direct sales – the practice of face-to-face demonstration, presentation and sale of services and products.

Downsizing – when a company reduces its workforce. Corporate downsizing is often the result of poor economic conditions and/or the company's need to cut jobs in order to lower costs or maintain profitability.

Electronic resume – a resume that is submitted to a potential employer electronically. The purpose of an electronic resume is to apply for jobs online.

Emotional Intelligence – the ability, capacity, or skill to perceive, assess, and manage the emotions of oneself, of others, and of groups.

Entrepreneurial – having the spirit, attitude or qualities of an entrepreneur: enterprising.

Facebook – an online social networking service. Its name comes from a colloquialism for the directory given to students at some American universities and has expanded to an older demographic as well as in business.

Following up – critical and perhaps most important task whether you are in sales or a job search. This is the process in which you follow up with a thank you note, phone call or 2nd meeting to keep a communication channel open until a decision is made.

Fortune 500 Company – one of the largest companies in the world. Fortune magazine annually ranks among the 500 largest companies, based upon revenue.

Franchise – a business established or operated under an authorization to sell or distribute a company's goods or services in a particular area.

Free Agent – an individual who considers his or herself equally dedicated to profession, network of professional contacts, and employers in proactively managing his career/livelihood.

Freelance worker – see Contingent workforce.

Full-time job – a job that normally consists of working at least 8 hours per day, five days a week and usually 40 hours per week.

Gainful employment - an employment situation where the employee receives meaningful, consistent work and fair payment from the employer.

Globalization – the process of international integration and exchange arising from the interchange of world views, products, ideas, and other aspects of culture.

Good economic times – a period in which economic activity increases (typically measured by Gross Domestic Product, 'GDP') and unemployment drops to a level that is considered 'full employment'.

Google – an American multinational corporation specializing in Internet-related services and products. These include online advertising technologies, search, cloud computing, and software.

Great Commission - the final command of Christ that is found in Matthew 28:18-20. This contains what has come to be called the Great Commission: "Therefore go and make disciples of all nations, baptizing them in the name of the Father and of the Son and of the Holy Spirit, and teaching them to obey everything I have commanded you."

Hard skills – skills that you learn over time or through your life. The skills you learn at school or through employment to perform specific duties are hard skills. Analytical, financial, computer programming are all examples of hard skills.

Headliner – a marketing term used to describe the 'catchphrase' or 'attention phrase' that, when defined and delivered correctly, results in getting the recipient to take action and keep engaged.

Hidden Job Market – a common term referring to "unpublicized," "unpublished," "unadvertised," or "unposted" job openings and considered to be in the majority of the way jobs are filled. These phrases are considered controversial in that it implies a conscious effort by employers to deliberately hide jobs from the public, which is likely not the case in most situations. It's most typically the void of time from when a job is conceived and determined to be filled, but before it's posted, at least in mid-sized and larger companies. However, it is true that some companies, particularly small ones, may never post.

Hit Submit Mentality – a term used to describe a way of thinking by a job seeker that by applying to each and every online job posting whether the posting is on a company's web site or on a recruiting site, makes the seeker feel he/she is being productive with their job search.

Humanistic capitalism – a concept that seeks to marry humanism, specifically the welfare, safety and health needs of people and the environment, with an embrace of market forces and a market-based economy.

Human Energy – the Energy Field, sometimes called the Aura, is a complex combination of overlapping energy patterns which define the unique spiritual, mental, emotional and physical makeup of an individual.

Industrial Revolution – the major technological, socioeconomic and cultural change in the late 18th and early 19th century resulting from the replacement of an economy based on manual labor to one dominated by industry and machine manufacturing.

Informational interviews – a meeting in which a potential job seeker seeks advice on their career, the industry, and the corporate culture of a potential future workplace.

Innovator's mindset – is a 'growth' mindset, in which one is oriented towards creating value in the marketplace. As a employee, it means creating solutions for things employers or consumers want or need; as well as creating new value by providing useful things they didn't even know they wanted.

IQ – a measure of a person's intelligence as indicated by an intelligence test.

Job Hopper – a job hopper is a term used to describe a person who finds it difficult to stay with a company for longer than a few months. In today's fluid job market, the term has essentially lost its meaning.

Joint Ventures – when two (usually well-established) companies join together on a project or investment.

Keyword Search – a process of finding popular search terms and subsequently using them to perform specific searches. In terms of job searching, recruiters and employers utilize keyword searches to sort and filter electronic and scanned resumes to find and select job candidates as part of the job selection process.

Knights of Columbus – the world's largest Catholic fraternal service organization. It was founded by the Venerable Father Michael J. McGivney in New Haven, Connecticut, in 1882, and named in honor of the navigator Christopher Columbus.

Layoff – the temporary or permanent removal of a person from his or her job, usually because of cutbacks in production or a corporate reorganization.

LinkedIn – the world's largest social networking website for people in professional occupations with around 100 million members, as of 2014, in the U.S. alone. Ninety-five percent (95%) of Recruiters use LinkedIn for sourcing job candidates.

LinkedIn Influencers – a group of over 300+ individuals who are considered Influencers because of some prior or existing success (innovation, product, service) that originated from their action. These influencers, also known as thought leaders, are allowed to share original content directly with LinkedIn users.

LinkedIn profile – a LinkedIn page that describes you: your career history, education, interests, and other related content you may want to publish on the Internet in managing your career.

Long-standing job – a job that has been 'stable and permanent'.

Long-term unemployed – a category of unemployed workers that includes those who have been unemployed more than 27 weeks and who are not counted in official unemployment statistics.

Marketing collateral – in marketing and sales, the collection of media used to support the sales of a product or service. For jobseekers, marketing collateral includes resumes, business cards, LinkedIn profiles, and personal marketing pieces.

Mentor – someone who offers their knowledge, wisdom, and advice to someone with less experience or knowledge, typically without compensation.

A mentor may be a friend, relative, or business acquaintance; someone who may be instrumental in helping another person reach his or her short-term and long-term goals. A mentor is similar to a coach, but he or she uses a broader, more holistic process. In contrast to mentors, coaches have professional training and qualifications and are usually paid for their services.

Mentoring – a process for the informal transmission of knowledge, social capital, and the psychosocial support perceived by the recipient as relevant to work, career, or professional development; mentoring entails informal communication, usually face-to-face and during a sustained period of time, between a person who is perceived to have greater relevant knowledge, wisdom, or experience (the mentor) and a person who is perceived to have less (the protégé).

Millennial – a person born in the 1980s or1990s, a member of Generation Y, a person reaching young adulthood around the year 2000.

Mind mapping – used as a study aid, for organization, problem solving, and decision making. A mind map is a diagram that represents words, tasks, ideas, or other things, linked and arranged around a central word or idea.

Networking – the act of building relationships with others for mutual benefit. Networking can be live, face-to-face or online.

Network Marketing – a type of business opportunity that is very popular with people looking for part-time, flexible businesses.

New Economy – coined in the late 1990's, refers to the impact of information technology on the economy. It stated that traditional measures of value were no longer valid because technology was changing the world so quickly and dramatically. Also known as the "Digital Economy," it implied that any company not embracing the Internet in a big way was doomed to fail in the future, and its mantra was "Gain market share at all costs."

New World of Work – represents the transformation from lifetime employment with one company to multiple employers and industries.

Master networker – a term used to describe an individual who is very good at developing and managing a large personal and professional network.

Offer-Negotiation Mindset – having and/or demonstrating a habitual attitude toward evaluating a job offer and proceeding into a dialog to produce an agreement that both parties can accept.

Old Employee Model – a term used to describe the environment and nature associated with lifetime employment with one company vs. New Free Agent Model.

Outsourcing – the contracting out of a business process to another party. Outsourcing includes both foreign and domestic contracting, and sometimes includes off-shoring or relocating a business function to another country.

Panel Interview – a type of interview in which you will meet with several individuals at one time, typically sitting around a conference table. Many of these interviewers will be your direct and indirect managers as well as supervisors and colleagues; they will take turns asking you prepared questions.

Part-time worker – a person who works less than 40 hours per week.

Passive candidate – describes a person who is inactive in job search, but possibly interested in new employment.

Permanent employee – known as 'regular' employees who work for a single employer and are paid directly by that employer. In addition to their wages, they often receive benefits like subsidized health care, paid vacations, holidays, sick time and contributions to a retirement plan. Permanent employees are often eligible to switch job positions within their companies. Even when employment is 'at will', permanent employees of large companies are generally protected from abrupt job termination by severance policies, like advance notice in case of layoffs, or formal discipline procedures. Permanent employment rarely means that an individual's employment is guaranteed throughout their working life in today's economy.

Personal attributes – traits that make up your personality, which define who you are as a person. For example, these could be personal attributes to describe someone: outgoing, extrovert, open. They are important because they are what make you who you are, what other people find in you that they may like or dislike.

Personal Brand – describes your professional reputation; it's how you as an individual are perceived by your professional surroundings, including potential employers.

Personal identity – what makes you unique? It is the distinct personality of an individual and is concerned with the persisting entity particular to a given individual.

Personal interview – a type of interview for you to share your understanding of the job, the ideas and values you bring to the position, your motivations for applying, your talents and weaknesses, and other aspects of your candidacy.

Personal Value Statement (PVS) – also known as the 30, 60 or 90 second elevator pitch that everyone should master (no matter what your status is). This is an inspiring statement of whom you are, what you do and, if seeking a job, how you provide value and/or make a difference.

Phone interview – an interview held over the phone rather than face-to-face. A telephone interview will usually be given to candidates who have passed the online application as the next step in the evaluation process.

Plan B – a job or plan that can supplement one's primary income source or serve as a pivot to a new occupation. In terms of career or occupation, a proactive individual can have a Plan B job or business to fall back on, in the event of job loss or career change.

Professional degree – defined as a degree that is academic in nature that prepares the student for a career within that degree's listing. For example, a degree in accounting is a professional degree because it prepares the student for a career in accounting.

Professional network – a type of social network service that is focused solely on interactions and relationships of a business nature rather than including personal, non-business interactions.

Recruiter – someone who seeks out and supplies members or employees to organizations for pay.

Restructurings – a reorganization of a company with a view to achieving greater efficiency and profit, or to adapt to a changing market. Often includes downsizing.

Resume – a written summary of one's life comprising of one's education, accomplishments, work experience, publications, etc.; especially, one used to apply for a job.

Revolving Door Concept – refers to the ongoing turnover of employees in the business world. Employees are hired to perform certain tasks and, due to a variety of reasons, become dissatisfied and seek out jobs with other companies that have more appealing benefits.

Scanable Resume – refers to a hard copy document that can be successfully scanned using technology (OCR=Optical Character Recognition; developed in the 1970s) that scans the content of a paper document as a graphic image and then converts it back to text.

SCORE - Service Corps of Retired Executives. SCORE is a non-profit association dedicated to helping small businesses get off the ground, grow and achieve their goals through education and mentorship.

Search Campaign – for the job seeker; this term is used to describe a detailed written series of actions that are to be executed to identify and land a specific job, contract, or occupation.

Self-assessment – the process of looking at oneself in order to assess aspects that are important to one's identity. It is one of the motives that drive self-evaluation, along with self-verification and self-enhancement.

Self-esteem – a term used in psychology to reflect a person's overall emotional evaluation of his or her own worth. It is a judgment of oneself as well as an attitude toward the self.

Self-marketing – defined as promoting either your 'self' or your product with no outside help from a public relations department. For example, many book authors who work with small publishers with no publicity budgets must self-market to get the word out about their book. They schedule their own visits to bookstores, pay for and create their own websites and participate in social media sites to garner attention for their work.

Self-promotion – to sell yourself to others; to politely promote your value to others.

Situation/Task/Action/Result (S.T.A.R.) – a technique utilized on resumes and in interviews to describe a results-driven personality. You should describe the Situation or Task, the Action you took and the Results that occurred as a consequence of your action. When constructed and delivered correctly, an individual will, on paper and in person, convey a proactive, energetic problem solver who gets the job done.

Slow economic times – a period in which economic activity slows (typically measured by Gross Domestic Product, 'GDP') and unemployment increases above a standard level.

Social media – interactive forms of media, such as LinkedIn, Facebook, Google+, Twitter, and Instagram, etc., that allow users to interact with and publish to each other, generally by means of the Internet.

Soft skills – the interpersonal skills a person has that demonstrate how a person relates to others. Some soft skills are active listening, empathy and conflict resolution.

Strategizing – to make a plan for achieving a goal. Steps typically involve researching, brainstorming, and modeling career or business issues.

TED Talks – a lecture series free on the Internet. "Riveting talks by remarkable people, free to the world" is their heading. They are short, informative lectures from some of the brightest minds on the planet. Criminology, ecology, robotics or nearly anything of interest is there. The talks are fairly brief and are meant to be for a variety of people so jargon is mainly avoided.

The Great Recession – a label used by journalists and economists to describe the severe, prolonged economic downturn of 2008/09. Some economists trace the Great Recession to the collapse of the United States housing market in 2007.

Transferable Skills – skills that you can take with you from one job to a completely different one. For example, as an engineering manager, a person has to demonstrate leadership skills that sometimes can be utilized in other industries.

Triple Bottom–Line (TBL) Oriented – in the private sector, a commitment to TBL implies a commitment to a business's material impact for good on the environment and people, in addition to profits. The triple bottom line has also been extended to encompass four pillars, known as the quadruple bottom line

(QBL). The fourth pillar denotes a future-oriented approach (future generations, intergenerational equity, etc.). It is a long-term outlook that sets sustainable development and sustainability concerns apart from previous social, environmental, and economic considerations.

U3 unemployment index – U.S. Bureau of Labor Statistic, which is the government's primary measure of unemployment. The index does not include all unemployed workers, such as those for whom unemployment benefits have expired or those who have given up looking for work.

U6 unemployment index – U.S. Bureau of Labor Statistic that attempts to capture both unemployed and under-employed individuals. It is a more complete snapshot of the job market, but research shows it is also much understated.

Unemployed – a person without a paid job and who is available for work.

Under-employment – describes the employment of people with skills and competencies that justify better pay and benefits than their current position provides. For example, someone with a master's degree and advanced accounting experience who is doing entry level accounting or part-time work.

Unemployment Insurance (UI) - a government program to help workers who have lost their jobs through no fault of their own. It provides temporary income until unemployed workers are able to find new jobs. Unemployed workers who quit their jobs voluntarily or were fired for a good reason are not eligible for weekly benefits. Benefits typically consist of 13 weeks, often extended by Congress to 26 weeks during sluggish economic times.

White collar workforce – a broad occupational grouping of workers engaged in non-manual labor.

"The New World of Work is fraught with both challenges and opportunities. Having faith, courage, and inspiration can lead to miraculous things for you, your loved ones, and your community."

DANA WALLACE GOWER

Business, Career and Wealth Strategist
Birth State: Maine

Dana has a diverse range of business experience spanning over 30 years. This includes work in both Human Resources and Financial Services. Prior to becoming independently employed, Dana served in various roles for global organizations including former Fortune 500 Cooper Industries and large insurers such as AXA Advisors and Lincoln Financial.

Dana holds an MBA in finance from top-ranked Rollins College in Orlando, FL and A.S./B.S. degrees from the University of Maine, one of the oldest land-grant universities in the U.S.

Dana lives in Cary, NC and is a proud father of 5 terrific kids and 6 wonderful grandchildren. He is a parishioner at St. Andrew the Apostle Catholic Church in Apex, NC where he is co-director of the Career Network Ministry.

Dana is a member of the Knights of Columbus, Council 6650 in Cary, NC. He is the co-author of the national seminar *Charting a New Course* and accompanying book, *The Career and Financial PowerBook for Job Transitioners*. In the past, he has been active with The Mankind Project, Boy Scouts, United Way, Rotary International, Financial Planning Association, Society of Human Resource Management, Junior Achievement, and Kappa Sigma Fraternity.

"Never stop learning. My father once told me that if you don't learn something new each day, then it was a wasted day. Treat each day as a fresh opportunity to learn something and find ways to help others realize how special they are."

VENARD PAUL DEAN
NC Registered Consulting Forester
Birth State: Alabama

Paul has over 30 years experience in diverse occupations, from Information Technology to Forestry.Experienced in multiple areas, he has served in software development and project management positions with IBM and Nortel Networks. He has managed the Information and Forest Management Departments of a multi-million dollar resort, and developed forest management plans for landowners throughout North Carolina.

Paul holds a B.S. degree in both Computer Science and Forest Management from highly-rated Auburn University.

Paul lives in Cary, NC where he is happily married to Barbara. They have two wonderful children, Andrea and Chris. He is a parishioner at St. Andrew the Apostle Catholic Church in Apex, NC, and he is the founding director of the Career Network Ministry.

Paul is a member of the Knights of Columbus, Council 6650 in Cary, NC and is an Assistant Scout Master for Boy Scout Troop 209 in Apex. He is a member of the Society of American Foresters, North Carolina Prescribed Fire Council, and Tau Kappa Epsilon Fraternity.

REFERENCES

[1] Solman, Paul (2013) PBS NewsHour: *Suicide and the Unemployed*

[2] American Community Survey (2008-2012 – 5 Year Estimates). Retrieved October 2014 from US Census Bureau http://www.census.gov/.

[3] National Employment Law Project, *Data Brief* (April 2014) Retrieved October 2014 from http://nelp.org.
National Employment Law Project, *Data Brief* (April 2014) Retrieved October 2014 from http://nelp.org.

[4] Saad, Lydia (2013) Gallup: *Majority of U.S. Workers Say Job Doesn't Require A Degree.* Retrieved from www.gallup.com/poll/164321

[5] Kessler, Glenn Retrieved January 2015 http://www.washingtonpost.com/blogs/fact-checker/wp/2014/07/24/do-10000-baby-boomers-retire-every-day/

[6] CBS News (June 2013). *Study: Most Americans unhappy at work.* – Gallup Study. Adams, S. (2012) *New Survey: Majority of Employees Dissatisfied.* Retrieved from www.Forbes.com.

[7] George, B. (2011). *Why Leaders Lose Their Way.* Harvard Business School: Working Knowledge; Washington Blog (May 2014). *Lack of Trust-Caused by Institutional Corruption – Is Killing the Economy*; Wikipedia (2014). *List of Federal Political Scandals in U.S.* Retrieved from www.Wikipedia.com.

[8] Foroohar, R. (2013). *Washington Dysfunction is Hurting GDP Growth.* Time Business & Money.; Davidson, K. D, (1985). *Megamergers: Corporate America's Billion-Dollar Takeovers.* Beard Books.

[9] Zalonski, P. (2014). *Category Archives: Pope Pius XII Saint Joseph the Worker.* Retrieved October 2014 from http://communio.stblogs.org/index.php/category/pope-pius-xii/

[10] Knights of Columbus. Retrieved October 2014 from www.kofc.org

[11] Domhoff, G.W., (2013*). Who Rules America? Wealth, Income & Power.* Retrieved October 2014 http://www2.ucsc.edu/whorulesamerica/power/wealth.html

[12] Various Authors. (2013). *The Bible: 50 Ways It Can Change Your Life Magazine.* Time Home Entertainment Inc.

[13] Caritas in Veritate. Retrieved July 2015 from http://w2.vatican.va/content/benedict-xvi/en/encyclicals/documents/hf_ben-xvi_enc_20051225_deus-caritas-est.html

[14] Wallis, J., (2010). *Rediscovering Values – On Wall Street, Main Street, and Your Street.* Howard Books.

[15] *The Editor's Desk – Annual Hires and Separations, 2012.* U.S. Department of Labor (DOL): Bureau of Labor Statistics (BLS)

[16] Hall, A., (2013). *I'm Outta Here! Why 2 million Americans Quit Every Month.* Forbes Magazine – Retrieved October 2014 www.forbes.com.

[17] *Employee Tenure Summary for January 2012.* U.S. Department of Labor (DOL): Bureau of Labor Statistics (BLS).

[18] Gayle, S. F., (2013). *Companies Turning To Tools To Manage Contingent Labor.* Retrieved October 2014 from http://www.workforce.com/articles/companies-turning-to-tools-to-manage-contingent-labor.

[19] Giang, V., (2013). *40% Percent of Americans Will Be Freelancers By 2020.* Business Insider. Retrieved October 2014 from http://www.businessinsider.com/americans-want-to-work-for-themselves-intuit-2013-3

[20] Pink, Daniel H. (2001). *Free Agent Nation The Future of Working For Yourself.* Warner Books Inc.

[21] U.S. DOL – Bureau of Labor Statistics (June 2014 data). *Alternative measures of labor underutilization – Table A-15.*

[22] National Employment Law Project, *Data Brief* (April 2014) Retrieved October 2014 from http://nelp.org.

[23] (A) U.S. *Unemployment: Three Million Jobs in America Are Waiting To Be Filled.* www.moneymorning.com (July 2013) (B) Needleman, Sarah E. *Skills Shortage Means Many Jobs Go Unfilled. Wall Street Journal Small Business* (July 2014)

[24] Gelb, Michael J. (2000). *How to Think Like Leonardo da Vinci: Seven Steps to Genius Every Day.* Bantam Dell, A Division of Random House.

[25] Robbins, Tony (1992). *Awaken the Giant Within: How to Take Immediate Control of Your Mental, Emotional, Physical and Financial Destiny!* Free Press, A Division of Simon & Schuster.

[26] Covey, Stephen R. (2004). *The 7 Habits of Highly Effective People: Powerful Lessons in Personal Change.* Simon & Schuster, New York, NY.

[27] Maltz, Maxwell M.D (1989) *Psycho-Cybernetics – A New Way to Get More Living Out Of Life.* ELCS. Pocket publishers.

[28] Burns, David M.D. (Orig. 1980) *Feeling Good – the New Mood Therapy* HarperCollins Publishers, New York, NY.

[29] (A) *The Energy Project.* www.theenergyproject.com – See Case Studies; (B) Mindset – *5 Ways To Improve Your Performance.* Exos.; Retrieved Oct 2014 from www.coreperformance.com ; (C.) Lawrence, T. Lavon (2012) *Mental Focus – You Are Only As Valuable As Your Mental Targets.* Retrieved Oct 2014 from http://www.neuro-sculpting.com/mental-training-blog

[30] Price, R.H., Friedland, D.S., & Vinokur, A.D. (1998). *Job loss: Hard times and eroded identity.* In J.H. Harvey (Ed.) Perspectives on loss: A sourcebook (pp. 303-316). Philadelphia, 23 PA: Taylor & Francis.

[31] Isaacson, Walter (2011). *Steve Jobs.* Simon & Shuster, NY, NY

[32] A. Amabile, Teresa & Kramer, Steven (2011). *Do Happier People Work Harder? NY Times*; B. Kertay, Dr. Leslie (2013). *The Bottom Line – The Happy Worker Prescription.* Chief Medical Officer, Lincoln Financial Group, Philadelphia, PA.

[33] Benedict XVI, Pope (2008). *Saved In Hope: Spi Salvi.* Ignatius Press San Francisco.

[34] Ouspensky, P.D. (1974). *The Psychology of Man's Possible Evolution.* Vintage Books Edition (p. 86).

[35] Madanes, Cloe (2013). *The 14 Habits of Miserable People – How to Succeed At Self-Sabotage.* Alternet www.alternet.org

[36] Lewis, Sarah (2011) *Positive Psychology at Work: How Positive Leadership and Appreciative Inquiry Create Inspiring Organizations.* Wiley-Blackwell.

[37] Morin, Amy (2014). *Positive Thinking Isn't A Substitute For Positive Action.* Retrieved July 2015 from http://www.forbes.com/sites/amymorin/2014/07/31/positive-thinking-isnt-a-substitute-for-positive-action/

[38] Joel, Billy (1985 - Song). *You're Only Human (Second Wind).* Columbia/Sony Music Entertainment.

[39] Career Thought Leaders Consortium, *Findings of 2012 Global Career Brainstorming Day: Trends for the Now, the New & the Next in Careers* http://www.careerthoughtleaders.com/wp-content/up/CTL-Brainstorming-Day-2012-Whitepaper.pdf

[40] Salovey, Peter & Meyer, John D. (1990). *Emotional Intelligence.* Baywood Publishing Co., Inc.

[41] Bramson, Robert M. Phd. (1981) *Coping With Difficult People.* Random House, Inc. NY, NY

[42] Cooney, Joe (2014) *Campbell's Chicken Noodle Soup: Looking good after 80 years.* Retrieved October 2014 from http://www.courierpostonline.com/article/20140117/BUSINESS20/301170008/Campbell-s-Chicken-%20Noodle-Soup-Looking-good-after-80-years

[43] Arruda, William & Dixson, Kirsten (2007) *Career Distinction: Stand Out by Building Your Brand.* John Wiley & Sons, Inc. Hoboken, NJ.

[44] Bennett, John Associate Professor (2011) *It's all About Who You Know: Networking to Get a Job* Retrieved from: http://www.foxbusiness.com/personal-finance/2011/04/25/know-networking-job/ ; Beatty, Kimberly (2010) *The Math Behind the Networking Claim.* Retrieved October 2014 from: http://blog.jobfully.com/2010/07/the-math-behind-the-networking-claim/ McIntosh, Bob (2012) *80% of today's jobs are landed through networking.* Retrieved October 2014 from: http://www.recruitingblogs.com/profiles/blogs/80-of-today-s-jobs-are-landed-through-networking

[45] MacKay, Harvey (2012). *Dig Your Well Before You're Thirsty: The Only Networking Book You'll Ever Need.* Crown Publishing House, a division of Random House, Inc. New York, NY.

[46] Carnegie, Dale (1998, 1936 Orig.). *How to Win Friends and Influence People.* Pocket Books, Simon Shuster NY, NY.

[47] Hoffman, Reid & Casnocha, Ben (2012). *The Start-Up of You – Adapt to the Future, Invest in Yourself, and Transform Your Career.* Crown Business, a division of Random House, Inc. New York.

[48] Granovetter, Mark S. (1973). *The Strength of Weak Ties.* American Journal of Sociology 78, no. 6: 1371

[49] Cooke, Phil (2012) *Shifting Your Productivity Mindset* Retrieved October 2014 from http://www.forbes.com/sites/work-in-progress/2012/08/16/shifting-your-productivity-mindset/

[50] Snyder, Phyllis & Barth, Michael C. (2013) *Taping Mature Talent – Policies for a 21st Century.* Workforce Council for Adult & Experiential Learning U.S. DOL

[51] Anthony, Mitch (2008). *The New Retirementality.* John Wiley & Sons, Inc. Hoboken, New Jersey.

[52] Skillings, Pamela (2008) *Escape from Corporate America: A Practical Guide to Creating the Career of Your Dreams.* Ballantine Books

[53] Bolles, Richard N. (2015, updated annually). *What Color is Your Parachute.* Ten Speed Press, Crown Publishing Group, division of Random House, Inc.

[54] Ancowitz, Nancy (2009) *Self-Promotion for Introverts: The Quiet Guide to Getting Ahead.* McGraw-Hill

[55] Van Grove, Jennifer (2013). *LinkedIn Member base climbs almost 40% in a year.* CNET. Retrieved October 2014 from http://www.cnet.com/news/linkedin-member-base-climbs-almost-40-percent-in-year/

[56] Smith Hyrum (2000) *What Matters Most - The Power of Living Your Values* Simon & Shuster, New York, NY

[57] Slaper, Timothy, Ph.D. and Hall, Tanya *The Triple Bottom Line: What Is It and How Does It Work?* Retrieved January 2015 from http://www.ibrc.indiana.edu/ibr/2011/spring/article2.html

[58] Toschi, Fr. Larry OSJ, Bertolin, Fr. Jose' OSJ, Sarkisian, Rick PhD (2012). *Husband Father Worker: Questions & Answers about St. Joseph* –Liguori Publications, Liguori, Missouri

[59] *NY Times* (1993) *First Layoffs Seen at IBM.* Retrieved from: http://www.nytimes.com/1993/02/16/business/first-layoffs-seen-at-ibm.html

[60] Hoffman, Reid & Casnocha, Ben (2012). *The Start-Up of You – Adapt to the Future, Invest in Yourself, and Transform Your Career*. Crown Business, a division of Random House, Inc. New York.

[61] Career Thought Leaders Consortium (2013). *Findings of the 2012 Global Career Brainstorming Day: Trends for the Now, the New and the Next in Careers.* White Paper Retrieved from http://www.careerthoughtleaders.com/wp-content/up/CTL-Brainstorming-Day-2012-Whitepaper.pdf

[62] Whyte, William (1956, 2002). *The Organization Man.* (Originally by Simon & Shuster, Inc.) University of Pennsylvania Press, Philadelphia, PA

[63] Johnson, Kevin (2013) *The Entrepreneur Mind: 100 Essential Beliefs, Characteristics, and Habits of Elite Entrepreneurs.* Johnson Media Inc.

[64] Beach, Jim; Hanks, Chris; Beasley, David (2011) *School for Startups: The Breakthrough Course for Guaranteeing Small Business Success in 90 Days or Less.* McGraw-Hill

[65] Riklan, Michele A. & David (2013) *101 Great Ways to Compete in Today's Job Market.* Self-Improvement Online Inc.

[66] Beckwith. Harry & Christine Clifford (2006). *You, Inc: The Art of Selling Yourself,* Warner Business Books, New York, NY

[67] Price, R.H., Friedland, D.S., & Vinokur, A.D. (1998). University of Michigan. *Job loss: Hard times and eroded identity.* In J.H. Harvey (Ed.) Perspectives on loss: A sourcebook (pp. 303-316). Philadelphia, PA: Taylor & Francis.

[68] Davenport, Barrie (2013). *Find Your Passion by Answering These 50 Questions* at http://www.barriedavenport.com

[69] Gallup survey (2013) *The 2013 State of the American Workplace* Report. Retrieved March 2015 from: http://www.gallup.com/services/178514/state-american-workplace.aspx

[70] Kelly, Matthew. *The Rhythm of Life: Living Every Day with Passion and Purpose* (2005). Beacon Publishing.

[71] John Paul II, Pope. *Laborem Exercens (On Human Work), #10.* Retrieved September 2015 from http://w2.vatican.va/content/john-paul-ii/en/encyclicals/documents/hf_jp-ii_enc_14091981_laborem-exercens.html

[72] CBS News (June 2013). *Study: Most Americans unhappy at work.* – Gallup Study. Adams, S. (2012) *New Survey: Majority of Employees Dissatisfied.* Retrieved from www.Forbes.com.

[73] Haydon, R. (2013). *Show me the money: The ROI of employee engagement.* DecisionWise. Retrieved from http://www.decision-wise.com/blog/2013/06/10/show-me-the-money-the-roi-of-employee-engagement/

[74] McPherson, Susan (2012) Harvard Business Review https://hbr.org/2012/01/why-csrs-future-matters-to-you

Notes & Thoughts

Notes & Thoughts

Notes & Thoughts

Notes & Thoughts

Notes & Thoughts